D0354140

"Goldie Hawn embodies delight and joy, and *10 Mindful Minutes* radiates these. Her book can help any adult—parent, grandparent, teacher—make double use of their moments with the children they love and have a terrific time while helping shape that child's brain for a lifetime of resilience and happiness."

—Daniel Goleman, bestselling author of *Emotional Intelligence*

"Goldie Hawn is arguably the most influential happiness expert of our time. She not only has achieved true happiness in her life but radiates it in her family and through the work of her foundation. Now, *10 Mindful Minutes* offers a guide for the rest of us. This book artfully blends the latest science and quick, easy how-to advice with a rare glimpse into the epiphanies that led to Goldie's happiness work. It's an engaging must-read for every parent interested in raising a focused, balanced, and happy child."

—Dan Buettner, *New York Times* bestselling author of
The Blue Zones and *Thrive*

"I saw how quickly the kids—and then the teachers—bought into the [MindUP] program and practices. The kids just got it right away, and seemed hungry for something that would help them manage the stresses in their life. . . . In my twenty years of measuring social-emotional learning quotients, I've never seen a program that works as well as this one."

—Dr. Kimberly Schonert-Reichl

"Goldie Hawn has given us a beautiful guide to one of our most important roles—raising healthy, joyful, and resilient children. Rooted in scientific research and chock-full of practical tools and techniques, *10 Mindful Minutes* will forever change the way you parent, and it'll change how you live your own life, too."

—Greg Hicks, bestselling coauthor of
How We Choose to Be Happy and *Happiness & Health*

10 Mindful Minutes

Giving Our Children—and Ourselves—the Social
and Emotional Skills to Reduce Stress and Anxiety
for Healthier, Happier Lives

Goldie Hawn

with Wendy Holden

A PERIGEE BOOK

A PERIGEE BOOK
Published by the Penguin Group
Penguin Group (USA) Inc.
375 Hudson Street, New York, New York 10014, USA
Penguin Group (Canada), 90 Eglinton Avenue East, Suite 700, Toronto, Ontario M4P 2Y3, Canada
(a division of Pearson Penguin Canada Inc.)
Penguin Books Ltd., 80 Strand, London WC2R 0RL, England
Penguin Group Ireland, 25 St. Stephen's Green, Dublin 2, Ireland (a division of Penguin Books Ltd.)
Penguin Group (Australia), 250 Camberwell Road, Camberwell, Victoria 3124, Australia
(a division of Pearson Australia Group Pty. Ltd.)
Penguin Books India Pvt. Ltd., 11 Community Centre, Panchsheel Park, New Delhi—110 017, India
Penguin Group (NZ), 67 Apollo Drive, Rosedale, Auckland 0632, New Zealand
(a division of Pearson New Zealand Ltd.)
Penguin Books (South Africa) (Pty.) Ltd., 24 Sturdee Avenue, Rosebank, Johannesburg 2196,
South Africa
Penguin Books Ltd., Registered Offices: 80 Strand, London WC2R 0RL, England

While the author has made every effort to provide accurate telephone numbers and Internet addresses at the time of publication, neither the publisher nor the author assumes any responsibility for errors or for changes that occur after publication. Further, the publisher does not have any control over and does not assume any responsibility for author or third-party websites or their content.

Copyright © 2011 by Rutledge Productions Inc.
Illustration on page 12 by Steve Karp
Text design by Tiffany Estreicher

First edition: October 2011

Library of Congress Cataloging-in-Publication Data

Hawn, Goldie Jeanne.
    10 mindful minutes : giving our children—and ourselves—the social and emotional skills to reduce
stress and anxiety for healthier, happier lives / Goldie Hawn with Wendy Holden.
    p.   cm.
Includes bibliographical references and index.
ISBN 978-0-399-53606-9
    1. Thought and thinking.   2. Awareness.   3. Relaxation.   4. Stress management.   5. Parent and child.
I. Holden, Wendy, 1961–   II. Title.   III. Title: Ten mindful minutes.
    BF441.H325   2011
    158.1—dc22   2011008297

PRINTED IN THE UNITED STATES OF AMERICA

10 9 8 7 6 5 4 3 2 1

Most Perigee books are available at special quantity discounts for bulk purchases for sales promotions, premiums, fund-raising, or educational use. Special books, or book excerpts, can also be created to fit specific needs. For details, write: Special Markets, Penguin Group (USA) Inc., 375 Hudson Street, New York, New York 10014.

To all parents who want to
let the light in their children shine.

CONTENTS

To bring up a child in the way he should go,
travel that way yourself once in a while.

—Josh Billings

FOREWORD

Goldie Hawn's career in the film industry has spanned almost four decades. Not only is she a beloved actor, but she has broken new ground as a producer or director of more than twenty films, worked in theater, and written a bestselling memoir. Yet with all of this success, Goldie's most intense passion has been in promoting the well-being and safety of children. From her early adult years to the present time, she has worked with various charitable and research organizations focused on the needs of children throughout the world. In her private life, Goldie is a devoted mother who has raised four children in what she describes as her most important role. She is now a grandmother, experiencing, in her words, the "opening of my heart with more joy than I can possibly express."

What I came to appreciate from firsthand experience is that Goldie is a thoughtful, creative, and intelligent person who is dedicated to bringing wisdom and warmth into the experience of how children develop. I was fascinated to discover that her long-standing public and private devotion to children and their well-being was being effectively channeled into the public school system with the MindUP program, which is supported by her foundation. This unique and scientifically based program is designed to help children learn "mindfulness"—a now proven way to help develop social and emotional intelligence. By training the focus of attention, the practices that form the MindUP program strengthen the mind and create more empathy and compassion within relationships. Mindfulness also builds stronger brains. More than just creating an innovative program, Goldie required that research demonstrate whether or not these educational strategies had a measurable impact. And they certainly did: not only did children experience enhanced attention and improved relationships, but actual biological measures demonstrated that they were able to handle stress in a healthier manner.

The Hawn Foundation's program also incorporates cutting-edge knowledge about the brain into its curriculum in an accessible and practical way, so that the students can use this information in their daily lives. MindUP is now being used in Canada, Great Britain, and the United States in increasing numbers of schools.

It is immensely satisfying to know that Goldie is interested in how perspectives from science, including studies of the brain, might support her program. Together Goldie and I presented a talk at a Technology, Entertainment, Design—Medicine (TED-MED) event and enjoyed an enthusiastic response to the idea of blending the ancient practice of mindful awareness with applications of modern science. Simply put, why not help kids develop stronger minds, not just fill their minds with facts? Why not

move beyond the basic three Rs of reading, writing, and 'rithme-
tic and add the fourth R of *reflection*—and even the fifth and sixth
Rs of *relationships* and *resilience*? This reflective approach has
also been presented to the nation's public school superinten-
dents and other organizations interested in helping children's
social, emotional, and academic intelligence.

From my perspective as both a mental health professional and
a parent, it seemed a natural next step for this work to be trans-
lated into practical exercises that anyone who cares for children
on a regular basis could use not only to teach their children but to
become more reflective themselves. Resilience, self-understand-
ing, and compassion are essential skills that can be learned. In
fact, learning and teaching these skills may be what is necessary
for us to shift the course of human evolution in a more positive
direction. Reflection is no longer a luxury but necessary for our
survival.

10 Mindful Minutes can change the direction in which society
is moving today by strengthening the minds of the next generation. In these pages you will find an educational (and entertain-
ing) narrative that provides the scientific grounding as well as
the practical strategies for developing your child's—and your
own—mindful awareness. You and your child can learn to live in
this new way: being aware in the present moment, letting go of
judgments and expectations, and being more fully available to
others and yourselves.

As *10 Mindful Minutes* demonstrates, you are the best teacher
for your child when you become a role model, showing your
child by word and deed the importance of paying attention, moment to moment. Mindful awareness is about being able to engage all of our senses—to taste the food we eat, to sense the air

we breathe, to listen with attention, to see with fresh and inquir-
ing eyes, to pause and appreciate the wonder of a butterfly your
child has discovered on the sidewalk before rushing off to school.
Learning to value even the most commonplace activities—and
finding the teachable moments in each of them—has the potential to make the ordinary quite extraordinary.

With practice we can transform this temporary state of
awareness into a lifetime habit. With just a regular ten-minute
practice, we can even improve the way in which our brains function. It only takes a few basic steps to transition from being on
automatic pilot to becoming awakened to present-moment experience. The practice then strengthens reflective learning into a
new way of seeing and being in the world.

There is magic in learning to use the mind to awaken our
lives. In my professional field, we use the term *mindsight* to describe the process by which we can learn how to focus our attention on the internal world of the mind in a way that will literally
change the wiring and architecture of the brain. This reflective
skill enables us to see and shape how our minds regulate information flow, how our brain circuits permit that flow to unfold,
and how our relationships share this flow of information as communication between people. Mindsight permits us to awaken
our lives and enhance the health of our mind, brain, and relationships. It is the key to emotional and social intelligence. In many
ways, *10 Mindful Minutes* offers you basic steps to learn not only
how to become more mindful in your life but how to enhance
mindsight in your family.

Studies of parent-child relationships reveal that one of the
most important factors in helping children thrive is the parents'
capacity to reflect on the internal world of the mind. Parents who

develop this skill can sense their own and their children's minds with more clarity. Scientific research in the field of attachment has revealed that parents who *see* the mind, think in mind terms, and communicate about the mind have children who develop well in the social, emotional, and cognitive domains. Children learn to know their own and others' mental landscape by the way we as parents, teachers, or other caregivers engage with them. The secure attachment that results from such mindsight-fullness serves as an "emotional vaccine"—a form of resilience for children as they grow. Naturally, we cannot guarantee the outcome of our children's development, but learning lessons from science about the power of reflection and communicating this power can give them the healthiest start possible.

As a father and child psychiatrist, I know both personally and professionally how challenging parenting can be. The last thing you need is yet another book to clutter your bedside stand or waste your time. But every lesson and every story in this book will make becoming mindful a bit more accessible to you. You'll find some basic yet important information about how the brain works in easy-to-digest nuggets, which will lead to understanding the workings of your child's mind and the forces that drive his or her behaviors. Equally important, you will find practical ways to model and teach mindfulness to your child. Along the way you'll discover—or rediscover—the power of gratitude to further promote well-being in yourself and your child.

Daniel J. Siegel, MD

ONE MOTHER'S JOURNEY TO MINDFULNESS

It is not enough to have a good mind;
the main thing is to use it well.

—René Descartes

THE PILOT

From the day my first child was born, I knew that I could not fail at one thing in my life—being a good mother. My most challenging and important role would be to help shape those little beings of pure potential.

Jobs, friends, and even spouses come and go, but your children are yours forever—even when they set sail away from the motherland. As they head out to sea, we begin to question ourselves: Were we always there for them when we were working so hard? Were we present enough at their soccer games, recitals, and birthdays, and when they were hurt or sick? Were we able to rejoice with them when they did well at school or mastered some new skill? Did we give them too much or too little? Did we pay attention enough to sense the things they weren't saying, to sense when they were hiding their anger, sadness, or pain? Ah, the myriad questions that run through our minds as we helplessly watch the vessel carrying our precious cargo sail into uncharted waters. The ship's pilot is left on the shore.

The analogy of the pilot is a good one, for it is a vital job on any vessel. We parents are here to guide, love, and nurture our children's emotional development so that they can set sail on their own adventure to happy, healthy, and productive lives. To be a good pilot is a daunting task in today's frenzied world. It requires focus, attention, and commitment. This is hard when often both parents are working full-time to make ends meet, technology is robbing the intimacy from family life, and so many other challenges keep us from being fully present for our children's safety and well-being. The demands of raising children can create more stress than we ever imagined possible. And yet, there can be no job or commitment more important than the emotional imprint we make on the babies we've brought into this world.

When I was a little girl, I longed for the day I'd become a mother. I brushed my doll's hair, fed her imaginary food, and sang her lullabies before tucking her into bed with me at night. I drew pictures of houses with white picket fences threaded with roses. The door to that house was always open, ready to welcome the children from the neighborhood. My vision seemed so perfect, and the life I imagined so easy. I was going to be the chef, the baker, and the homemaker; my days would be filled with happiness and joy. What an idyllic dream. Guess what? Things didn't turn out that way.

My firstborn, Oliver, nearly died at birth. My second baby,

Kate, was a year old when her father and I divorced, creating even more uncertainty and sadness. That's when I discovered that children are nothing like dolls and that being a parent is really hard. Even fame and fortune can't make those things better—in fact, they can make raising children that much more challenging. My most joyful discovery at this difficult time was that in spite of the enormous responsibility of nurturing my children, my heart not only grew larger but seemed to expand until it could hold a limitless amount of loving-kindness.

Sometimes, though, even a mother's love isn't enough. Being a single parent was challenging, as I tried to juggle my responsibilities and working demands with being there for my children. I even became an assistant soccer coach, though I barely knew the rules of the game. I can laugh about that now, but the tears came at night when I'd lie alone in bed wondering what happened to my perfect dream. Would I ever find a man to love, who would love me and, most of all, love my children as I do? It seemed impossible, and then a miracle happened. I met Kurt Russell. Kurt came into our lives and swept us up in his nurturing paternal arms. He brought his son, my stepson Boston, with him to make us a real family. Wyatt was born three years later—the final strand threading us together. I am now the proud grandmother to Ryder, Wilder, and Bodhi, with another baby on the way. I have the family I always dreamed of having. Miracles can happen. I look at my children and am amazed that—after all the trials and tribulations we went through together—somehow we made it.

Being a mother called on me to use many tools, some that I had and some that I didn't. I was fortunate enough to have had very good parents who, despite both working full-time, engaged and supported me. Most of all, they loved me. They were the most wonderful parenting role models, but even that wasn't enough. I still had a lot of unanswered questions. And the search for answers led me to greater awareness in understanding my own psychology and in learning how to quiet my own mind and to focus my attention.

I realized that I had to become the role model I wanted for my children. I had to be brave and look at myself truthfully. This wasn't easy. Stripping yourself bare and finding out what you're really made of is an important moment. Once you absorb the clarity and truth of who you are, you discover the empathy and understanding to help guide your children through their own journey of self-discovery.

THE FLAG

It was an ordinary weekday morning like any other. The telephone rang and a girlfriend told me, "Turn on the news." I switched on the television and watched, openmouthed, as two New York skyscrapers crumbled. My immediate thoughts were for my kids. My fourteen-year-old, Wyatt, was getting ready for school. Kate and Oliver were both in Los Angeles. And Kurt, too. We were all safe.

Like relatives at a deathbed, we gathered together in front of the TV—watching, waiting, and weeping. With each new image and every slow-motion replay, we mourned the passing of life as we had known it. This was real. This was a game changer. The world would never be the same after this. The events of 9/11 would polarize people of every country, religion, color, and creed. Reactions would ripple back and forth across oceans, creating a tidal wave of suspicion and fear. I saw the future unfolding before us, and it frightened me.

My mind flashed back to a day when I was eleven years old. At school I'd excitedly skipped down the hallway to the classroom on Visual Aids day thinking we were going to see a movie on agriculture or the arts. To my surprise, the film started with a big clock counting down from nine to zero. Then a booming voice announced, *"This is what will happen if there is an enemy attack!"* Up on the screen appeared scenes of annihilation and death. This was a civil defense film on what would happen if an atom bomb hit America. We children were supposed to crouch under our desks, cover our heads, and turn away from the blinding light. "Duck and Cover" was the message.

The world as I thought I knew it changed in that instant. My young brain was forever imprinted with horrific images I couldn't begin to understand. My body began to shake uncontrollably and I started to cry. Panicked, I fled from the classroom and ran home. Sobbing, I telephoned my mother, who rushed home from work and eventually calmed me down.

That childhood experience never really left me. For a long time afterward, I'd have to stay home from school if the town sirens went off during a drill. The seed of fear the film planted grew into a deep-seated terror that blossomed into fully blown panic attacks well into my young adulthood. Physically affected by my secret anxiety, I was afraid even to voice it and so was left to suffer in silent distress.

As I watched the events of September 11 unfold some forty years later, I wept. I knew this event would certainly traumatize the tender minds of children watching an American flag fluttering in the smoking ruins. How could they possibly understand?

How would these images and the fear they carried inform their future?

I went to my knitting basket and found some old threads of red, white, and blue. Knitting has always been a form of meditation for me, and so I began to knit the American flag. As I sat there, tears falling onto my stitches, I came to a profound and deeply emotional decision. I felt compelled to do something, no matter how insignificant, that would be more meaningful and lasting than the joining of a few fragments of wool.

My kind of patriotism doesn't have to do with being red or being blue; it doesn't even have a label. It has to do with loving my country and its great potential and respecting our powers of resilience. No matter how small a gesture, I believe that we can all do something to make this world a better place.

If I could help just one little girl or boy move beyond those images that will haunt us all, that would be a gift. Remembering my own childhood anxiety, I longed to show children everywhere how to rediscover their natural joy, understand the value of their emotions, and learn to feel empathy for others. I had no idea how to set about achieving this, but I knew as I knitted that I had to figure something out. Maybe it wasn't happiness I could bring our children; maybe it was hope. Either way, I felt compelled to try.

MY QUEST

I have always been fascinated by the power and resiliency of the human spirit, and as a person still on a lifelong journey of self-discovery, I set about my quest. I began to attend conferences and seminars on neuroscience and what is known as "heart-mind education." My search opened up to me a whole new world about how our brains work and the way they respond to information dependent on our emotions.

I discovered that the landscape of the mind is an endlessly fascinating place. The more I learned, the more excited I became about tapping into its almost limitless potential. Not only did researchers and scientists give us undeniable proof that the human brain is a living, growing organ, but their findings also gave rise to the notion that we can choose to change the way we interact with the world, starting with the mind, to give us the best out of life. They proved that when we—or our children—are stressed, anxious, bored, or unhappy, we are much less able to cope with problems and take in new information. Our brains close tight like a clenched fist. If we are happy, relaxed, and curious, on the other hand, our brains open like a flower, and not only does this help us to remember and properly process information but it also gives us the ability to handle stress.

Along this path to greater understanding, I met some incredible innovators who shared my vision for the well-being of our children. They kindly invited me into their extraordinary world. These experts soon became my teachers and my guides. With their help and inspiration, in 2003 I set up the nonprofit Hawn Foundation, which went on to initiate a social and emotional learning program in elementary schools called MindUP. We chose to focus on schools because these are the places where children spend most of their young lives. By creating a community in the classroom, especially for those without a lot of support at home, we hoped to provide a safe haven imbued with optimism and joy.

The essence of MindUP is that children learn the simple biology of their own brains. While schools routinely teach children to memorize the names of every major bone and muscle in their bodies, from the tibia to the biceps, they are taught very little about the brain—the most important "muscle" of them all. Through the MindUP program, they learn how the emotional part of the brain can hijack the more clear-thinking areas that keep us calm and focused. Discovering the mechanics of the brain helps children understand where their emotions come from. It allows them to become more self-aware and empowers them to manage and reduce their own stress. It effectively puts them in control of the way they respond to the outside world.

Once they have grasped brain basics, they are taught how their thoughts and feelings affect their behavior. They discover the effects breathing has on the brain. They learn how to appreciate the sensory aspects of their lives and what responses they evoke. Finally, they explore their emotional states and are taught social and interpersonal skills. In a way, MindUP tends to children's souls.

Once we'd established the core principles, we asked some of the best brains in the scientific world to help us create a program that could be integrated into the regular school curriculum. Then we sent our specially trained staff out into schools nationwide. MindUP has now grown to cover North America and the United Kingdom and is introducing joyful learning and brain-friendly strategies into what we are calling "the optimistic classroom." In order to educate the whole child, we are bringing what we call "the fourth R" to education after reading, writing, and arithmetic—and that is *reflection*. And as Dr. Dan Siegel says in his foreword to this book, "Reflection is no longer a luxury but necessary for our survival."

In short lesson extensions that serve to enhance the learning experience, children are encouraged to do the following:

■ Learn how their brains react to emotions, so that they can bring themselves back to a neutral point

■ Take daily "brain breaks" and focus on breathing

■ Practice mindful sensing—exploring sight, taste, smell, hearing, and motion

■ Consider the differences between optimism and pessimism

■ Learn to savor happiness

■ Engage in practical problem-solving and critical thinking

■ Learn perspective and how to view differing results

■ Focus on compassion and empathy

■ Discover the importance of generosity and a sense of social responsibility

■ Perform random acts of kindness

In this groundbreaking approach, the program applies all these activities to the academic and curricula standards that teachers are obliged to meet. This is really what makes MindUP so accessible for the teaching staff because the program is integrated and isn't simply an add-on. This seems to work for the children, too, as various studies have shown.

THE RESULTS

The Hawn Foundation funded research to measure the effectiveness of the MindUP program. The results proved to be very positive. I was delighted to learn that a majority of children in one study reported that what they loved most about MindUP was that it helped them learn how to make themselves happy. This study was conducted by Dr. Kimberly Schonert-Reichl of the University of British Columbia.

Here are some of the findings from the study:

- Better reading scores

- Less absenteeism

- A 25 percent reduction in aggression on the playground

- Better attention and more concentration

- Quicker reactivity in answering questions and responding to teachers

- Better interpersonal relationships

- Improved ability to manage stress

- A 63 percent rise in optimism among participants

In a study of more than 200,000 children in similar programs, CASEL (Collaborative for Academic, Social, and Emotional Learning) found that classroom behavior was improved and students were more engaged in learning. There was a decrease in depression and an increase in the ability to control emotion. There was even a reduction in the likelihood of drug use, and because emotional and social skills play a critical role in academic performance, test scores were up. Students in social and emotional learning (SEL) programs ranked at least ten percentile points higher on achievement tests than those who were not.

Another study replicated the results and found that children in the MindUP program were rated to be the following by peers:

- Kinder

- More trustworthy

- Helpful

- Better liked

- Less likely to break rules or start fights

MindUP children had greater working memory and ability to adjust to change. In fact, mindful practices were shown to stimulate the part of the brain responsible for good judgment and decision making.

Yet another study tested samples of saliva for levels of the primary stress hormone cortisol, which goes up and down naturally during the day. Released in the body as a direct response to stress, cortisol has been linked to everything from heart disease to cancer. Through focused awareness, MindUP children were able to bring their cortisol levels down throughout the day, indicating that they were better able to manage stress. This is a truly valuable skill because stress interferes with memory. When we can lower our cortisol levels, we are able to concentrate more and have greater powers of recall. When a child's brain is frenzied or stressed, it is very difficult for him or her to learn or retain information. When a child is full of enthusiasm and inspired by wonder, it's a beautiful seeding ground for learning.

"I must say I was skeptical at first," Dr. Schonert-Reichl told me. "But I was surprised when I saw how quickly the kids [fourth and fifth graders]—and then the teachers—bought into the program and practices. The kids just got it right away and seemed hungry for something that would help them manage the stresses in their life. . . . In my twenty years of measuring social-emotional learning quotients, I've never seen a program that works as well as this one. I had to go back and look at the numbers again to be sure."

This news was thrilling. What had started as a flicker of an idea on the darkest of days had blossomed into a bright reality. MindUP had achieved so much of what I'd hoped for. The testimonials of parents and teachers (many of which appear in this book) only encouraged me further, as they told me children were taking the practices home to teach to their families. In fact, one little girl shared a story with me that was quite funny. She told me her mother was taking her to school one day and, as she put it, "there were thousands of traffic and cars everywhere," and her mother was cussing and yelling and anxious, rushing to get her to school—at which point the little girl leaned over, looked at her mother, and said, "Mom, take a deep breath, relax, do your mindful breathing, and maybe you won't say so many bad words."

THIS BOOK

Thanks to the success of the MindUP program, I have met countless parents eager to know more and to carry its positive influence into their family life. So many moms and dads, even those who didn't have children in the program, claimed they needed to learn these tools, too, and asked me questions like: How can *we* become calmer? Can *we* learn to be less reactive? Where can we find out more?

> *MindUP really helped me basically with a lot of things, like sleeping through the night, eating, being happier at school, making new friends, and blocking out my little sister's nagging!*
>
> —William, age 12

And so it was that I came to write this book. I am not an expert, and I am most certainly not a scientist. It would take years for me to understand the symphony of the brain. But what I have discovered so far is truly exciting. Now I hope to share with you the genius of those who have dedicated their lives to the fields of social and emotional learning and positive psychology in the hope of giving our next generation a brighter future.

It's not for me to tell anyone how to manage their lives or even how to bring up a child. I am not a perfect parent, but that doesn't mean I shouldn't strive for perfection. What I do know is that MindUP works for children, so its principles can work for parents, too. I hope to help us all become more aware, manage our own stress, and become fully present in our own lives and those of our children.

I've always thought that the perfect metaphor for good parenting is the advice given by airlines to put on your own oxygen mask before assisting your children with theirs. The same applies to being a parent. We need to gain the strength we need along with the awareness and intention to give the best possible start to our children. By adopting a more mindful approach and learning to quiet our own minds and reduce the effects of stress, we'll be more in control of our own emotions and reactions. This will help us not only in our parenting but also in all our personal relationships, in the workplace, and in the world at large.

A peaceful, happy child is the first step toward a peaceful, happy world. I hope that with this book I can help parents put their own emotional struggles in proper perspective and allow them to reconnect with the tickle of happiness we all have inside.

By lifting the veil on the joys of parenting, we can share in the wonder of not only making the most of our brains but also growing our hearts. We *can* be the role model of all that we wish for our children. We *can* create optimism and focus in ourselves and our children. We *can* nurture their sense of well-being and ability to be aware of and control their states of mind. We *can* bring a sense of comfort to our lives and give our children compasses with which to navigate the world once they leave our shores.

Children are a small part of our now but one hundred percent of our future. My mission is one mother's attempt to foster happiness, success, and emotional literacy in those who will inherit our world with all its beauty and flaws. By fostering the same in ourselves, we can lead by the example of our own joyfulness and peace of mind.

Please join me in this crucial task. From the bottom of my heart, I thank you for helping the light inside your child shine.

Goldie Hawn

The Experts

The material presented in this book is just the beginning. Those who've guided us have written far more deeply on this subject, and I urge you to read what you can of their work from the bibliography at the end of the book. I've done my best to explain what they have discovered and how we can incorporate it into our daily lives. (There is also a short glossary at the end of the book for quick reference.)

The experts who have kindly agreed to share their findings and insights with me are doctors and practitioners, neuroscientists and psychologists. They are also mothers, fathers, aunts, uncles, and grandparents who—like me—want to help find the best ways to raise a healthy human being. Anybody who loves children and is worried about the way our society is heading only has to look at the extraordinary results of their work. And once we study the science, then the directions become clear.

I have cited many experts in this book, but the following are those whose research and encouragement I have found most helpful, and whose most important and relevant findings appear throughout:

Daniel Amen, MD, assistant clinical professor of psychiatry and human behavior at the University of California, Irvine, School of Medicine and author of *The Amen Solution* and *Change Your Brain, Change Your Life*, among other books

Sharon Begley, scientific journalist and author of *The Plastic Mind* and *Train Your Mind, Change Your Brain*

Mihaly Csikszentmihalyi, PhD, positive psychologist and director of the Quality of Life Research Center, Claremont Graduate University

Richard Davidson, PhD, professor of psychology and psychiatry, University of Michigan, and founder of the Center for Investigating Healthy Minds

Adele Diamond, PhD, neuroscientist at the University of British Columbia and one of the founders of development cognitive neuroscience

Daniel Goleman, PhD, psychologist and author of *Emotional Intelligence* and other books

Amishi Jha, PhD, professor of psychology, University of Miami

Jon Kabat-Zinn, PhD, professor of medicine emeritus and founding director of the Stress Reduction Clinic and the Center for Mindfulness in Medicine, Health Care, and Society at the University of Massachusetts Medical School

Susan Kaiser Greenland, PhD, teacher, founder of the Inner Kids mindful awareness program, and author of *The Mindful Child*

Linda Lantieri, MA, expert in social and emotional learning, CASEL (Collaborative for Academic, Social, and Emotional Learning)

Madeline Levine, PhD, psychologist and author of *The Price of Privilege*

Helen Neville, PhD, professor of psychology and neuroscience, director of the Brain Development Lab, and director of the Center for Cognitive Neuroscience, University of Oregon

Kimberly Schonert-Reichl, PhD, associate professor of education, University of British Columbia

Daniel J. Siegel, MD, associate clinical professor of psychiatry at the UCLA School of Medicine and codirector of the Mindful Awareness Research Center

Kathryn Wentzel, PhD, professor of human development, University of Maryland, Maryland Literacy Research Center

Judy Willis, MD, MEd, neurologist, teacher, and author of *How Your Child Learns Best*

Why We Need to Act Now

The mind is like a parachute—it works only when it is open.

—Frank Zappa

LOSING JOY

A baby smiles between fifty and seventy times a day, and a toddler approximately six hundred times, according to research. I'm sure some of us have asked ourselves where that smile goes. What robs us of it? This chapter sets out the alarming facts about how our children are losing their happiness, too. It shows that these are desperate times for which we need an urgent call to action.

According to UNICEF, the children of the United States are the second *least* happy children in the world, after the United Kingdom, a fact that should shake every one of us to the core. How can it be that two of the most affluent countries in the world should have such a dismal record when it comes to being happy? Happiness is not a frivolous notion; it is a serious business. Every one of us has the right to be happy and to feel contentment and well-being. Making the intention to find our happiness even in turmoil is the first step to rediscovering it. Sadly, there are more worrying statistics that support some very uncomfortable truths.

Emotional challenges: As many as 8 percent of our children are believed to have emotional problems. The U.S. Public Health Service estimates that 6 to 9 million American children have a diagnosable mental disorder that impairs daily functioning. By their teens, as many as 20 percent are suffering from problems such as attention deficit/hyperactivity disorder (ADHD) and attention deficit disorder (ADD).

Depression: Infants as young as three years old are being diagnosed with depression. Some studies suggest that the rate of teenagers suffering from depression may be as high as one in eight. The American Academy of Child and Adolescent Psychiatry (AACAP) puts the figure at around 5 percent of the younger population.

Use and abuse of pharmaceuticals: There has been a 68 percent increase in pharmaceutical use to treat emotional disorders in girls and 30 percent in boys in the past decade, and the figures are escalating annually, according to the American Psychiatric Association.

Poor academic performance: Fifteen-year-olds in the United States place twenty-third in the global ranking of student performance on reading, twenty-eighth in mathematical literacy, and twenty-seventh in scientific ability, according to the latest Organisation for Economic Co-operation and Development report (2003).

Dropout rates: Forty-eight percent of our children do not graduate high school in the fifty largest cities, according to America's Promise Alliance.

Suicide: Suicides among adolescents have quadrupled since the 1950s. In 2009, an estimated 8 percent of high school children reported trying to take their own lives, and 17 percent reported "seriously considering" killing themselves, according to figures released by the U.S. Centers for Disease Control and Prevention. Statistics from the AACAP show that suicide is now the third leading cause of death in young adults aged fifteen to twenty-four, outnumbering homicides three to two. It is the sixth leading cause of death for five- to fourteen-year-olds.

Diminishing happiness: As many as 60 percent of our children feel chronically disengaged from school. In one study, 61 percent of fourth graders agreed with the statement "I am happy with life." By the seventh grade, only 36 percent made the same claim.

SUFFERING UNSEEN

Many of the children who are most at risk are those without a syndrome or a label. Their suffering is either unseen or unattended to, and they need help. Affluent children, in particular, are in trouble. They are either micromanaged to within an inch of their day or showered with material goods to make up for physical or emotional absence. This can lead to a sense of feeling misunderstood and empty. These children sometimes describe themselves as "bored and boring." Lacking resilience, they feel unable to cope with even minor setbacks. Without enthusiasm, they become apathetic. These children just go through the motions.

Many end up self-medicating with alcohol or drugs to get through the day. They have been labeled "the lost generation of neglect."

Suniya S. Luther, professor of psychology and education at Columbia University, who conducted a series of studies on resilience and vulnerability in teenagers, says that substance abuse and adolescent emotional problems, far from being inner-city issues of the poor and underserved, are found to be highest in suburban affluent groups, especially among girls.

Whether aged seven or seventeen, children are very good at hiding their true feelings from us, especially when much of what they feel stems from our expectations of them or from our neglect through our own preoccupations. It is natural for us to have high hopes for our children's well-being and happiness, but we must be careful not to fixate on what's wrong about them more than what's right about them. Sometimes we do fixate on their test scores; however, some children do not test well—they can be very smart, very creative, and yet have very poor test scores. Oftentimes children choke because of nerves, which diminishes their capability for critical thinking and memory. It is important to be mindful of the stresses our children face every day of their young lives. We must look below the surface and attune to them, so that we can quickly recognize the symptoms of their quiet distress and know how best to handle it. Isn't that all we ever want for our children—for them to be happy?

Reflections

The son of a dear friend of mine was caught cheating at school along with several others. For some reason, he was singled out. After being summoned to the principal's office, she watched her boy crumble as he confessed to what he and ten fellow students had done. Afterward, she and her son wept together in her car. She could see how confused, guilt-ridden, and hurt he was. "Everyone cheats, Mom," he cried. "We're afraid of failing or of not getting A's or B's." He lamented that the school had programs for children who took drugs or drank too much. "They need to have something for cheating, too, because everyone cheats and everybody's scared." When she told me this story, I fully appreciated the stress levels of our children and how pressured they are to succeed. No one was looking at the bigger picture of why normally well-behaved students would risk expulsion to break the rules and cheat. Maybe it's because of parental expectations, maybe it's because of the school's expectations. Or perhaps it's because these students felt their own need to appear as smart as some of their friends. Emotional literacy is just as important as academic literacy, if not more so. This kind of behavior is a marker of emotional illiteracy and can continue through to adulthood if not handled correctly.

The Wonders of the Brain

Once children realize that their minds matter, it makes a
difference to how they'll learn. It reinforces the enjoyment
and impact of the experience of learning.

—Daniel J. Siegel, MD

DISCOVERING THE POWERS OF THE BRAIN

We are living in such exciting times—when parents, teachers, and government officials all recognize that the old paradigms aren't working. We now know that we have to rethink how we nurture the next generation and improve our children's emotional lives (or their emotional intelligence, to use the term popularized by Daniel Goleman). The future is in our hands, and soon to be in theirs.

Before we can fully embrace mindfulness in all its many facets, we need to understand a few key facts about the human brain. By becoming familiar with the chief structures involved in thinking, learning, and feeling, we can learn to use the powers of the brain to create emotional well-being. More important, we'll be able to explain to our children how the brain works, in simple ways, finding teachable moments to share our discoveries—at the dinner table, in the car, or on the way to school—whenever and wherever it feels appropriate. Most important, we can teach them that they can be in control of their brains rather than the other way around.

The pioneers in the study of neuroscience, behavior, and emotions are working in a constantly evolving and expanding landscape. The task of selecting the most up-to-date and relevant research and the most practical techniques for applying these findings to everyday problems has not been without its challenges. But I hope to distill their work and show how the brain and emotions—as well as the ability to focus, manage stress, and learn—are all exquisitely interconnected. And the best place to start is by first defining the fields of research in which the scientists and educators consulted for this book are working. Then we can go on to explore the mechanics of the brain itself, relating the hard science to its application in our everyday lives.

COGNITIVE NEUROSCIENCE

Modern-day studies of how the brain develops and functions have been enhanced by the use of neuroimaging devices like EEGs, MRIs, and PET scans, with which we can actually *see thinking* as it happens. These colorful computer images of the brain show us what happens to blood flow and electrical activity when someone is in a state of high emotion or in a state of peaceful calmness. These images give us a glimpse of an inner world we've never previously been able to see and give neuroscientists direct proof of cause and effect.

SOCIAL AND EMOTIONAL LEARNING

How we cope day to day with thoughts, feelings, emotions, and our connections to others has been the subject of intense scrutiny in the last few decades. What we are beginning to understand is that emotional intelligence—and a related idea, Emotional Quotient (EQ)—is at least as important as IQ.

Those who have higher social and emotional skills have been proven to function better in the world, regardless of their intelligence.

There are five basic sets of competencies that make up what is defined as social-emotional intelligence:

- **Self-awareness:** knowing what we think and feel, and how thoughts and feelings influence actions and choices

- **Self-management:** learning how to handle challenging emotions so that they don't cause problems; being able to set goals and deal with obstacles

- **Responsible decision-making:** being able to come up with solutions to problems and consider the consequences of actions on ourselves and others

- **Social awareness:** understanding the thoughts, feelings, and perspectives of others and developing empathy

- **Relationship skills:** being able to work through conflicts; having strong connections to other people but resisting negative peer pressure

POSITIVE PSYCHOLOGY

A relatively new field of study, positive psychology begins with the premise that it is more beneficial to promote mental health than to focus on the negative aspects of mental illness and other emotional problems. According to the University of Pennsylvania's Positive Psychology Center, founded by Dr. Martin Seligman, who is recognized as the father of the modern movement, "Positive Psychology is the scientific study of the strengths and virtues that enable individuals and communities to thrive. . . . Positive Psychology has three central concerns: positive emotions, positive individual traits, and positive institutions. Understanding positive emotions entails the study of *contentment* with the past, *happiness* in the present, and *hope* for the future. Understanding positive individual traits consists of the study of the strengths and virtues, such as the capacity for love and work, courage, compassion, resilience, creativity, curiosity, integrity, self-knowledge, moderation, self-control, and wisdom. Understanding positive institutions entails the study of the strengths that foster better communities, such as justice, responsibility, civility, parenting, nurturance, work ethic, leadership, teamwork, purpose, and tolerance."

> *By making data pleasurable and sensory, with games and activities, you can actually redirect the flow into the higher-thinking brain.*
> —Judy Willis, MD, MEd

Positive psychologists believe, in fact, that there is an innate human drive to want to lead a meaningful and fulfilling life. And it is their aim to build a science that supports families and schools that allow children to flourish, workplaces that foster satisfaction and high productivity, and communities that encourage civic engagement.

MINDFULNESS

The last but by no means least field of study that I include here can be considered one of the positive experiences cited by the proponents of positive psychology. But mindfulness is also an essential means to achieving fulfillment and happiness. Mindfulness is the conscious awareness of our current thoughts, feelings, and surroundings—and accepting this awareness with openness and curiosity in a nonjudgmental way. It means focusing our attention on *nondoing*, a crucial skill in these distracted times. It is more important than ever to teach ourselves and our children how to concentrate, so that we'll become aware when we've lost focus and be able to maintain our attention for longer periods of time. By discovering the wonders of such techniques as mindful breathing, which helps create a balanced neurological system, we can provide the perfect climate for healthy brain function.

> *Research suggests that people with higher levels of mindfulness are better able to regulate their sense of well-being by virtue of greater emotional awareness, understanding, acceptance, and the ability to correct or repair unpleasant mood states. . . . The ability to skillfully regulate one's internal emotional experience in the present moment may translate into good mental health [in the] long term.*
>
> —Jeffrey M. Greeson, PhD

How the Brain Works

*Education is discovering the brain.... Anyone who
does not have a thorough, holistic grasp of the brain's
architecture, purposes, and main ways of operating is
as far behind the times as an automobile designer
without a full understanding of engines.*

—Leslie Hart, *Human Brain, Human Learning*

The brain, along with the spinal cord and nervous system, controls all mental processes and physical actions. It is an incredibly complex structure, with almost infinite parts working in harmony to perform these mental, physical, and emotional functions.

For simplicity's sake, we'll describe the brain in the most general terms but concentrate on those aspects that relate more or less directly to mindful awareness.

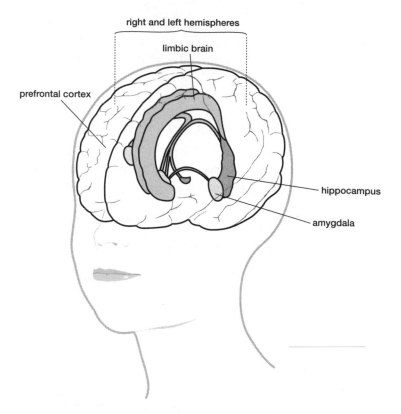

amygdala: an almond-shaped structure that acts like a Guard Dog in the brain

hippocampus: part of the limbic system that helps with memory and spatial navigation

limbic brain: also known as the emotional brain, a key area for emotions, long-term memory, and behavior

prefrontal cortex (PFC): the Wise Old Owl at the front of the brain, where our higher or critical thinking occurs

reptilian brain: the oldest part of our brain, also known as the "Stone Age brain," manages our automatic responses such as eating and breathing

right and left hemisphere: the two halves of the cerebral brain, linked by the corpus callosum

THE HEMISPHERES

The most obvious part of the brain—and perhaps what comes most immediately to mind when we think of the brain—is the cerebrum, the largest part of the brain, which is divided into *right and left hemispheres*, with a bridge between them. The two halves of the brain are always conversing back and forth across that bridge, but each hemisphere processes information differently and has a very distinctive role.

Some of us are led more by the *left hemisphere*, which is primarily responsible for linear, logical, and language-based thinking. This side specializes in understanding right from wrong and cause and effect.

The *right hemisphere* is more visceral and is responsible for holistic, nonlinear thinking. It specializes in intense emotions, visual and spatial information, sending and receiving nonverbal signals, and giving us a sense of ourselves and others. Children are primarily right-hemisphere thinkers, ruled by their emotions, which sometimes makes it difficult for parents (operating primarily from the left hemisphere) to reason with them. The left hemisphere kicks in around the age of four, which is when logic and the ability to put words to feelings start to develop, and parents are better able to reason with their children in what might be called a more rational, logical, and "adult" way.

By about age eight, the two sides of our brain begin to communicate better with each other. Also around this age we begin to show our innate tendency to favor one side of the brain or the other, depending on our temperament. If we are artistic and creative, then there is little point in trying to force us into left-brained activities or shape us into becoming something that we are not, and vice versa. For instance, I'm left-handed (hand preference is a function of one hemisphere's dominance over the other), and fortunately no one tied my left arm behind my back to force me to use my right, as was often the practice when I was small.

But when it comes to finding fulfillment and satisfaction in our emotional lives, operating too exclusively from one hemisphere or the other can be problematic. What we can achieve with mindfulness is a balance between the two sides.

THREE BRAINS IN ONE

From the outside, the brain may appear to be one great lump of bumpy gray matter, but hidden beneath the cerebrum are layers of the brain, or what might be called three brains in one:

1. The "Stone Age" or *reptilian brain* manages our automatic responses, such as eating and breathing.

2. The "emotional" or *limbic brain* is responsible for generating emotions and turning on and off our stress responses. Located deep in the center of the limbic brain is the *amygdala*, which acts like a Guard Dog at the gates of the brain. Its function evolved over millions of years, from the time of the saber-toothed tigers when we had to make decisions on whether to fight, take flight, or freeze. As the amygdala filters incoming information, it decides if it represents a threat or not. Once it determines that a threat is im-

> Many parts of the brain work together to produce complex behavior.
>
> —Richard Davidson, PhD

minent, it will fire up and release *stress hormones*, such as adrenaline and cortisol, which unleash the symptoms of fear and anxiety. These hormones are toxic and can stay in the body for several days. The amygdala also releases glucose to our muscles in preparation for action. If, however, the amygdala reads incoming information as pleasurable or safe, it will relax and open a kind of floodgate that allows data to move on up to the next level, the prefrontal cortex, where most critical thinking occurs.

3. The "new" or *cortical brain* plays a key role in memory, attention, perceptual awareness, thought, language, and consciousness. The biggest part of the cortical brain is the *prefrontal cortex (PFC)*, located right behind the forehead. The PFC is like a Wise Old Owl that observes, analyzes, and remembers information. It is in charge of the *executive functions*—thinking, planning, reasoning, problem solving, decision making, and impulse control. In other words, it controls most of what we think of as intelligence.

> The amygdala is where the heart meets the mind and emotional significance is linked to the data received to evaluate its pleasure value.
>
> —Judy Willis, MD, MEd

Proportionally, humans have the largest prefrontal cortex of any mammal. One of its most important roles is to regulate the signals emitting from the amygdala—in effect, calming down the Guard Dog in what Dr. Daniel Siegel calls "the dance between the mind and the brain."

Reflections

When my two eldest children were in primary school, I became increasingly aware that they were losing their way in the educational system. They seemed overwhelmed by rote memorization techniques and pressured by potential failure. I felt they needed to be engaged in a way that would make learning more joyful. Taking a deep breath, I went to see their principal to ask if she could help my children connect in a more personal way to their subjects, something I believed they needed. Thankfully, she was receptive to my ideas and began to implement some of them. In a subsequent English project, for example, the children were asked to photograph their families and write about them, which brought their history alive. I knew nothing back then about how the brain worked, but I did have an instinct. All parents have this gift, the ability to recognize their children's struggle if they just stop, observe, and pay attention. Only then can they help ease that struggle, no matter how little they know about the brain or understand the way emotions can color their children's day.

POSITIVE AND NEGATIVE

While the physical brain itself may be the starting point for all physical and mental functions, relaying information throughout the entire system would be impossible without the release of *neurotransmitters*—chemicals such as dopamine, serotonin, norepinephrine, and melatonin, which carry messages across the small spaces between brain cells. Dopamine, for example, which is of particular relevance to social and emotional learning, doesn't just help information pass more easily; it also gives us a pleasurable sensation. In fact, the mere thought of an enjoyable experience can release dopamine, in the same way that visualizing a chocolate cookie or other favorite food can make us salivate. Similarly, whenever we think a happy thought or recall a pleasant memory, dopamine is emitted and makes us feel more positive. Scientists have shown that dopamine can be released by acts of kindness and expressions of gratitude. Also, the release of dopamine helps with focus and memory—as you have probably experienced when working on a project that you really love or recalling a particularly pleasant experience.

The most important years for the growing brain are from birth to age six (although it doesn't finish growing until around age twenty-five). From our first breath, our brains are like little sponges soaking up everything around us. This is when parents are in a position of most influence because the positive and negative experiences the brain encounters have the most effect. It works like this: Electrical signals travel along the estimated 100 billion nerve cells in the brain known as *neurons* to form thoughts, memories, and feelings. With each new experience, the electrical currents fire in a certain sequence. The more often they fire, the more likely they'll be to fire in the same se-

> *Dopamine produces a feeling of alertness, attentiveness, quick thinking, motivation, and mental energy. Fear of failure, isolation, and stress cause dopamine to be converted into norepinephrine. This causes alertness to be converted into aggression and agitation, frustration, and apathy. Under such circumstances, how can children learn?*
>
> —Marc Meyer, PhD

quence the next time. Eventually the brain "wires up," creating deeper pathways. If we have negative thoughts, the brain fires more negatively, and vice versa. Just as our skills in riding a bicycle or playing the piano improve the more we do it, we can create healthier brains through positive practices such as mindfulness.

As living organisms giving off waves of energy, we have enormous, unseen power over those around us, especially our children. Even babies can pick up on our feelings via specialized brain cells known as *mirror neurons*. We become a mirror to our children. When we smile, they smile back. If we cry, they feel sad. This is why one of the key skills we need as mindful parents and teachers is to be aware of the emotional impact we have on our children. Whenever we embody calmness and happiness, we help create a calmer, happier, and more emotionally intelligent child. When we are frenzied, aggressive, or stressed, we can create similar behavioral problems in our children. This mirroring process proves how vitally connected we are as human beings. We feel each other, we entrain each other, and we need each other. It is not only making a connection with our children that matters but the quality of the connection we make.

The truth is that children not only copy what their parents are doing but also are "wired" to crave their parents' love and attention. This crucial connection between us is called attachment. What we want to create for our children's emotional, physical, and intellectual well-being is known as *secure attachment*—the belief that we're a safe harbor to shelter them from life's storms.

Creating secure attachment with your child is important because it fosters trusting and lasting relationships. Parents of securely attached children tend to play with them more and react more quickly to their needs. Studies have shown that secure children are more empathetic and less disruptive during later stages of childhood. Children with strong secure attachment tend to grow up with good self-esteem, are comfortable sharing feelings with friends and partners, and seek out social support.

Reflections

My mother was always very active, full of personality, and quite funny, but when I was about ten years old, she took to her bed for what seemed to be no reason. I was confused and worried. But she assured me that she was okay—she just had pain in her leg. Soon I, too, started to feel listless. I didn't want to go to school, and believe it or not, my leg hurt, too. My mom eventually took me to the doctor because she thought that the pain in my leg might affect my dancing, which was a big part of my life then. The doctor asked me to do an *entrechat*, which is a jump in the air, to show him my ballet moves. I did so happily, completely forgetting the pain in my leg. He looked at my mother, whom he had also been treating, and said, "Your daughter is experiencing sympathetic pain." My mother recovered quite quickly after that. I think that when she realized I was mirroring her experience, she fought whatever had been ailing her, and her leg stopped hurting. Magically, so did mine. We are so much more deeply connected than we think.

By the teenage years, children are a battleground of mixed emotions. Physically, their brains are only half grown. They are being subjected to a wave of hormones. They may appear surly, disgruntled, and embarrassed by our presence, but as research has found, they're secretly comforted by their parents' company because their preadolescent brain still craves the attention of those they love. In other words, in spite of appearances, the teen is still seeking secure attachment.

During the teen years, another extraordinary thing is happening in the brain. Just as we prune roses to create healthier plants, the brain prunes old connections it isn't using anymore. And as we may sometimes snip the wrong stem and affect a plant's vitality, the brain can do the same thing, losing information along the way. Dr. Judy Willis describes it as "a physical reshaping of the brain in response to experience."

> The research shows that relationships with parents can change, and as they do, the child's attachment changes. This means it is never too late to create positive change in a child's life.
>
> —Daniel J. Siegel, MD

Parents can become frustrated and angry at not understanding teenage behavior, but this is one of the times when their role is so vital. Coupled with the hormonal onslaught that happens in the teenage years and the ongoing pruning process, our growing children have few powers of judgment or reasoning at this time. To make matters worse, they feel invincible. This is when they are most susceptible to outside influences, good and bad.

The bad news is that substance abuse at this tender age can permanently alter the brain's development. According to recent research published in the *Proceedings of the National Academy of Sciences*, binge-drinking teenagers can do lasting harm to the parts of the brain that relate to memory and the formation of mental images. They also set up addictive patterns that can last a lifetime.

Understanding that the teen brain is quite literally rearranging itself minute by minute explains much of what we experience with children of this age. We look at them and wonder who they are. But I would suggest they don't really understand themselves at this point. By being kind, attentive, and patient, we'll help them navigate through this most difficult period so that they can eventually flourish. The lessons you learn in this book will help you handle anything their mixed-up teenage brains throw at them, and at you. Mindfulness—both yours and theirs—is the key to success.

> *If children believe that external "stuff" will alleviate emotional distress, they go on to think the same about drink, drugs, or sex. It becomes a quick fix . . . but teen brains are notoriously sensation-seeking, with no impulse control, and vulnerable to toxins. Drink and drugs will effect changes in their brains, which can worsen into psychiatric conditions in later life. Even marijuana affects attention, memory, and processing of information.*
>
> —Madeline Levine, PhD

Reflections

Puberty was a roller-coaster ride of emotional ups and downs for me. One minute I'd be so happy I'd want to burst out of my skin. I'd close my bedroom door and sing and dance and pretend I was on a Broadway stage. Then at any given moment throughout my day I would get a sinking feeling as depression and sadness came over me. It was so strange. I didn't understand it. How could I be so up one minute and so down the next? The only consolation was that my girl-friend had those moments, too. We even had a code for what we were feeling. We'd call it the TFs, which stood for Terri-ble Feelings. We had each other, and we gave our problem a name. We shared this experience, so we didn't feel so alone. I recall those feelings so vividly and, of course, now know that they were hormonally induced. The beautiful thing is that we can use the memory of what it was like to go through those hormonal shifts and changes in dealing with the frustrations within our blossoming teens.

TECHNOLOGY AND THE BRAIN

Adults and children alike have become adept at multitasking—or so we like to think. We have to be, to keep up with the demands of life in the twenty-first century and the explosion in the use of technological and communication devices. Our children's appar-ent ease with video games, cell phones, and computers is a by-product of our brave new world and is thought by many to be an indicator of greater efficiency.

Communication and even friendship have gone online. We are barraged by information coming at us in a million byte-size pieces, challenging our ability to focus. With a diminishing atten-tion span in the face of such bombardment, we have developed the tendency to skim rather than give any one piece of datum deep thought. Our minds become like butterflies flitting from subject to subject, which impairs our ability to apply ourselves to a single task.

For young brains especially, this mental restlessness can have an enormously negative impact. In fact, the blitz of information from digital media can become intoxicating. For today's "screenagers," these flickering images are like bright diversions in the digital candy store. The need for them can become compulsive and often addictive. We have all become subject to a sense of urgency in which everything needs to be dealt with immediately. We are guilty of expecting our emails or texts to be answered immediately. Just as eating too many candies has a negative effect on our bodies, so the onslaught of unfiltered information can be damaging to young minds. Numerous studies have found that working memory is impaired, performance suffers, and the brain tires more easily as a result of being overwhelmed by relentless stimuli.

As we rely increasingly on machines to communicate, we lose the ability to interact in person. We are by nature social animals, and sharing intimacy with friends and family has tremendous emotional and physical benefits. But instead of talking to people directly, we find ourselves sending electronic messages. And when our children see us behaving this way, they copy us in a manner that puts them at risk of becoming unable to fully experience true intimacy and emotional contact.

> *The development of the prefrontal cortex appears to be profoundly influenced by interpersonal experiences. This is why our early relationships have such a significant impact on our lives.*
>
> —Daniel J. Siegel, MD

Aside from the emotional impairment, this "butterfly brain" approach is highly detrimental to our ability to focus. Nicholas Carr, author of *The Shallows: What the Internet Is Doing to Our Brains*, says, "We are evolving from being cultivators of personal knowledge to being hunter-gatherers in the electronic data forest." Lila Davachi, a neuroscientist at New York University, has found that the modern greed for digital media has a severe impact on cognitive function, especially memory. She and her team used an fMRI scanner to study the brains of a group of adults while they were examining photographs. Those who were asked to stop, lie still, and let their minds wander after their initial examination were found to have improved recall about the photographs than those who weren't instructed to do so. "Our data suggests that if you are not giving yourself a break," she reports, "you are hindering your brain's abilities to consolidate memories and experiences."

> *Teenagers feel so disconnected they look for well-being and connectedness in other ways, through sex, drugs, and alcohol.*
>
> —Jon Kabat-Zinn, PhD

Doctors at the Capio Nightingale Hospital in London, England, have a name for our increasing reliance on social media and all things technological: "e-diction." And they are even offering courses for sufferers who want to escape the sense of always being "tired but wired." Dr. Nerina Ramlakhan, a sleep and energy-management specialist at the same hospital, says, "Technology can cause addiction, burnout, and sleep problems, and people need to reflect on how they use it to ensure it doesn't become a problem."

A brain accustomed to static and noise while taking in information will develop the need for fast-paced input to even register in the future, according to leading child psychiatrist and brain-imaging specialist Daniel Amen. Are we inadvertently raising a generation with an addiction to thrill-seeking brain function?

Could this ultimately lead to dangerous, thrill-seeking behavior? Some at the American Academy of Child and Adolescent Psychiatry think so. They have found that many young people self-medicate with anything from marijuana to Ecstasy or inhalants as a means of escaping from their problems. The use of marijuana and alcohol in high school has become common. The average age of first marijuana use is fourteen, and alcohol abuse can start as young as twelve years old. A young brain made restless by an increased use of technology will not be so easily satisfied by an environment that seems flat or boring by comparison. Drugs and alcohol are quick ways to liven things up.

> Attention is the holy grail. Everything that you are conscious of, everything you let in, everything that you remember and you forget, depends on it. . . . Too much digital stimulation can take people who would be functioning okay and put them in a range where they're not psychologically healthy.
>
> —David Strayer, PhD

Dr. Gary Small, professor of psychiatry and biobehavioral sciences at the University of California, Los Angeles, and author of *iBrain: Surviving the Technological Alteration of the Modern Mind*, says, "Many studies have found an association between more time with technology and a lower attention span." While he reassures us that surfing the Internet is not always the demon it is made out to be and doing so uses as many if not more parts of the brain than reading a book, he distinguishes between *digital natives* (those born to technology) and *digital immigrants* (those who have come to computer technology as adults) and claims that there is a *brain gap* between generations. This gap—like all gulfs between different ages and groups of people—can cause alienation and isolation unless dealt with mindfully. Patience and openness to understanding allows communication, compassion, and empathy.

While we may never leave the world of computers, PDAs, and electronic games behind, what we and our children need is to reconnect with the simple pleasures of life. In logging off, taking our child's hand, and wandering outside to stare dreamily at the clouds or explore the backyard, we will encourage creativity and imagination as well as enhance well-being. More and more studies are finding that a return to nature is an effective and simple antidote to technological addiction and its detrimental consequences. It gives us the mental freedom to recalibrate our senses and refresh our minds. At the same time, we will be rediscovering the joy of human contact and shared intimacies.

Whether we are in the great outdoors or in a similarly calm environment indoors, once we are fully in control of our faculties we perform optimally and effortlessly. We are then able to tune back in to our body's natural rhythms. Psychologist Dr. Mihaly Csikszentmihalyi calls this optimal state "flow" and says it helps us feel happy, strong, connected, and motivated. Most of us have experienced what it is like to be in the moment when we are doing something so emotionally stimulating that we lose all track of time. We forget to look at our watches or check our electronic message systems—and we don't even care. I call it "rubber time" because minutes seem to stretch and the hours melt away.

> *Inner work teaches us that despite all the things that happen outside our control, our responses still mean that we can author our own lives.*
>
> —Jon Kabat-Zinn, PhD

Wouldn't it be nice if we could all experience rubber time every day—and the sense of motivation and connectedness that goes with it? Imagine if our children were bubbling over with excitement to tell us what they've learned or seen. How satisfying would it be if they were *eager* to go to school every morning and looking forward to each new challenge? How would it be if *we* were? Regardless of any academic aspirations we might have for our children, we want them to find their "flow" by nurturing their natural talents and feeding their innate curiosity within a framework of discovery, compassion, and self-reflection.

Without such balance, our children risk losing themselves in digital media and disappearing into a world where we can't follow. If we don't pay attention and monitor them to see how long they are spending on the computer, texting, or in front of the television, then we are not setting them any parameters or letting them know how destructive such addictive patterns of behavior can be.

The "single biggest chunk of waking life of the American child" is spent in front of a television or video screen, according to the American Medical Association. A television remains switched on in the average U.S. home for just short of seven hours every day. Even day care centers have the TV on as background distraction. Here are some other alarming statistics about the viewing habits of Americans from market research company AC Nielsen:

- Some preschoolers watch as much as twenty-eight hours of TV a week (the average is twenty-two hours).

- Over the course of a sixty-five-year life span, the average American will have spent nine years watching TV.

▨ By the time a child is eighteen, he or she will have watched an estimated 25,000 hours of television; witnessed more than 200,000 acts of violence, including 16,000 murders; and seen more than 20,000 thirty-second TV commercials. Imagine what that does to the brain. This kind of media saturation has been found to affect focus, reduce the amount of time spent reading, and lead to lower grades. Sitting at a desk or on a couch leads to lethargy and obesity. Spending large amounts of time playing video games can also create poor social skills and alienation.

Research has shown that children who watch violent movies or play violent computer games do not always become more violent, as many might assume. Some, of course, do imitate the violence they see by exhibiting more aggressive behavior. Others simply accept violence as a way to handle problems. For the majority, something worse happens. The emotional part of the brain is desensitized, reducing its capacity for empathy. According to the AACAP, children become "immune," or numb, to the horror of violence.

It is this desensitization that worries me the most because it leaves us with the prospect of an entire generation without the ability or desire to care for others. That's terribly dangerous because it will bleed into every aspect of their lives. Empathy is vital for both healthy relationships and a productive society. It is well documented that children who are socially responsible, trust their classmates, and solve interpersonal problems in adaptive ways do far better in life than those who do not.

It is not overly dramatic to state that our children's emotional well-being—as well as our own—is on the line. We need solutions that simultaneously promote social and emotional skills, mental health, and academic performance. The latest research indicates that these last two are closely interconnected: mental health affects academic performance, and academic performance affects mental health. All we want for our children is for them to find joy, get along with others, pay attention, solve problems, and deal with stress. In fact, we want for them what we want for ourselves—emotional fitness.

Reflections

I loved the time in which I grew up. There were fewer distractions of modern technology to steal my focus or cloud my imagination. My girlfriend and I used to sit on our front stoop and imagine what we would do next. We were creative in our play. We made up songs. We searched for rocks that we would then crack open to see the beautiful crystals inside. We lay on the grass and stared at the clouds, watching different shapes morph into faces or animals. We laughed for no reason. In the summer we sold lemonade and chocolate chip cookies. In the fall we raked all the leaves on our street into a pile and, one after the other jumped into the heap, laughing. To this day I still remember the pungent smell of the earth. That's what my childhood was like. Even now, I can relive them

> *To authentically teach someone, it's helpful also to be a student of the techniques yourself. Your child will learn best through your example and modeling.*
>
> —Linda Lantieri, MA

in my mind as if they were happening today. They bring me peace and happiness and, most of all, return my spirit to a profound sense of inner contentedness and well-being.

We adults lose our focus just as easily as children and experience the same overload whenever we become stressed-out. Many of us feel overwhelmed by the demands of technology, which can lead to depression. The good news is that we, too, can learn to attune to ourselves and become better role models for our children. Without such awareness, we are set adrift. With it, we have a strong anchor and can find a safe haven for a stable, resilient, and cohesive family.

By embodying mindful qualities in rediscovering the nature of our own happiness, we can become a model to our children. It would be wonderful if children knew how to be happy and chart their course naturally in life, but it doesn't always happen that way. Thanks to the pioneering work of the world's neuroscientists, however, we are finally getting some answers.

STRESS AND THE BRAIN

Stress appears to be a curse of our generation, blamed for so many ills. "I'm stressed-out right now," we say, or, "The stress is really getting to me." We all speak of stress as something that falls upon us like a sickness we can't control.

> *The stress response can become more damaging than the stressor itself, especially when the stress is purely psychological.*
>
> —Robert Sapolsky

Now that we are more aware of how our brains work, we can fully appreciate that once the amygdala perceives something as dangerous, it goes into fight, flight, or freeze mode. This flips on the stress response and shoots adrenaline and cortisol through the bloodstream, putting the body on alert, which will compromise our health if not managed.

Cortisol is an especially dangerous stress hormone, not only because of what it can do to our health but also because it limits the access to the prefrontal cortex, preventing us from thinking rationally. When we are in fight, flight, or freeze mode, here's how the body reacts:

- The heart starts to pound faster.

- Breathing becomes more shallow.

- Muscles tighten.

- Blood pressure and blood sugar rise.

- Perspective and the ability to see options are obscured.

- Digestion and immune systems are compromised.

The stress hormones in animals are very important—in fact, they are lifesavers. Animals survive in the wild by reacting to the stress response and attacking a predator, running away, or hiding.

While most of us are now living in relatively safe environ-

> [Stress] handicaps our abilities for learning, for holding information in working memory, for reacting flexibly and creatively, for focusing attention at will, and for planning and organizing effectively.
>
> —Daniel Goleman, PhD

ments without predators, the stress response can turn on automatically no matter what the perceived danger. It can arise during relationship problems, money worries, or difficult living conditions—none of which may be actual threats to our lives, but the brain does not always distinguish. (If you remember how you reacted during the last scary movie you saw, you'll realize how your thinking mind has to overcome the amygdala's more or less automatic response to danger. We have to consciously tell ourselves: it is only a movie!) Allowing the stress response to take over chronically can have disastrous effects, from heart disease, high blood pressure, lowered immune function, and the death of brain cells to the growth of stomach ulcers and other gastrointestinal issues. Uncontrolled response to stress depresses energy levels and alters eating patterns, which can lead to eating disorders. More disturbing still are the findings of one study that showed that ongoing stress *shrinks* the executive function areas of our brains and *stimulates* the habit-forming parts that keep us repeating actions in a negative pattern.

Unmonitored stress responses don't help us when we're in conflict with our child, boss, or partner because it is precisely during such times that we need our most rational minds to figure out solutions. As we learned earlier in this chapter, if the amygdala senses danger and releases the stress hormones, the flow of information to the prefrontal cortex, where rational thinking and emotional regulation take place, is impaired. In other words, our minds are hijacked. (More on this later.) Similarly, if our children go to school stressed, they won't be able to engage, absorb, or retain information. In fact, research has

Short-term stress lasting as little as a few hours can impair brain-cell communication and memory.

—Tallie Baram, MD

shown that chronic stress can shrink the hippocampus, the part of our brain that holds memory. So, unless we're faced with a genuine emergency, it is to our advantage to learn to stay calm and focused.

THE CHANCE TO CHANGE

More good news from the world of brain science: *you can teach an old dog new tricks.* It was once believed that the brain was shaped for life in childhood in a process called *neurogenesis,* and that the adult brain could not grow new neural pathways or brain cells. While the brain itself may stop growing by our midtwenties, we now know that neurogenesis still occurs in the brain well into our seventies and beyond. Researchers Peter Eriksson of the Sahlgrenska University Hospital in Göteborg, Sweden, and Fred Gage of the Salk Institute in San Diego, California, used a chemical marker that traced the development of new neural pathways in people of all ages and found that environmental enrichment helps neurogenesis. Further, according to a study by Elizabeth Gould of Princeton University, learning enhances neurogenesis, and stress inhibits it.

> *Plasticity relates to the growth of new neural connections and the pruning of unused ones. It is a physical reshaping of the brain in response to experience. . . . When more connections form there is a chance for greater learning.*
>
> —Judy Willis, MD, MEd

The phenomenon, known as *neuroplasticity,* means that we can change the structure of our adult brains and even our behavior at whatever age we are just by intentionally focusing our attention.

Just as an injured brain adapts by mapping out new neural pathways, so brain circuits for the regulation of emotion and attention are "malleable by the environment and are potential targets of training," says Richard Davidson, one of the world's leading brain scientists. Using an fMRI scanner, Davidson has shown that compassion meditation, even in short-term practitioners, induces significant changes in patterns of functional activity in the brain. Davidson believes that, in time, mental exercise will be accepted as something that is as important to general well-being as physical exercise.

It is so empowering to know that we can create whole new pathways to better choices and happier feelings at almost any age. We don't have to be victims of unhealthy mental habits from the past, especially not when we are teaching ourselves and our children new tricks.

Getting the Most Out of This Book

Children are like wet cement.
Whatever falls on them makes an impression.

—Haim Ginott

So far, you've learned something about the brain and how to use that information to bring context to some of the issues in your life. You have come to understand the power of parenting and the way we shape our children's brains. The rest of this book offers a combination of theory and practice.

The pages ahead offer some simple and highly effective ways you and your children can learn the techniques you need. By following easy mindful practices that can take as little as ten minutes out of a busy day, you can develop ways of managing your emotions and become more in the moment and closer to your children.

Most of the core practices are designed to be done with children between five and twelve years old, but that's only a guide. You know the abilities and interests of your children better than anyone else, so take advantage of what's happening in their lives and tailor the practices to their ages and personalities. The more relevant you can make them, the more engaged your children will become. With older children, it helps to tell them how excited you are to learn these things with them because you are taking a journey together.

Try to make it fun, keep it light, and enjoy the spirit of play. Especially in the beginning, your children may giggle or fidget, but that is entirely normal. Let them have their own responses and experiences, even if you think they should react differently. Try to respond positively. One study showed that if a teacher smiled when she gave a lesson, her pupils remembered more than if she hadn't. An optimistic, open environment is ideal for healthy growing and learning.

Reflections

Every evening when I came in from school, my father would ask me, "Hey, Go, what did you learn today?" Or he might say, "How was your day, on a scale of one to ten?" I loved that question because it allowed me to reflect on my day. In his own quiet way, my violin-playing, madcap inventor of a dad made me mindful of my blessings. He made me look at the bigger picture, something I try to continue to do as part of my daily mindful practice.

We all know that something as simple as playing "I Spy" in the car with our children not only creates a time of sharing but also helps them focus on an objective. The games and exercises in this book help strengthen the mind muscles in a similar way.

Each section focuses on a specific topic, such as mindful breathing or how to deal with difficult emotions, and then spells out easy ways that you can best utilize the practices. Once you're set with a core practice, then what follows will help you deepen and broaden the experience at a time and pace that suits you.

Repeated practice is both crucial for learning and vital to building new pathways in our brains to the behaviors we want to develop.

Our goal of becoming more mindful with our children doesn't have to become another chore or burden that needs any special preparation. Read through the chapters quietly and familiarize yourself with all of them to get a better overall grasp of the information. Or choose the sections that focus on what you believe are the key needs for you and your children. Once you feel comfortable with the core practices and are ready to share them, figure out when would be the best time and place to try them. It could be at the dinner table or out in the yard playing ball. You'll know best.

I found that the hour at which I tucked my children into bed at night was a beautiful time, and I liked the idea of them going to sleep with positive thoughts in their heads. You can also suggest that your children use the practices whenever they need to during the day. As they go off to school, for instance, you might suggest they draw on their mindful breathing if ever they feel angry or frustrated. Then, when you're at work and feeling similar emotions, you, too, can implement what you have learned. In this way, you can build a family culture around these ideas.

Eventually these teachable moments will become a natural

part of daily life. Even after that challenging day when we feel we've left little pieces of ourselves all over the place, these tools will help gather those bits back into place. Know that the work you'll be doing here will set you on a better path. Time spent with your children strengthens the connection between you and has a value that cannot be measured.

Remember the joy you felt inside when you were small, because we need to be ever mindful of the child within us when we're using the practices in this book. We can all still share that joy with our children so that we never break their spirit. Sometimes by remembering and sharing with them our own memories we can amplify the experience.

I used to walk to school by myself every day, play outside until dark, and wait for my mother to call me in for dinner. How different that is from today. Children are monitored continually and driven everywhere. Fewer and fewer venture outside alone. Overloaded with as much homework as they have schoolwork, they have their precious hours divided into time slots—not to mention all the after-school programs, sports, play dates, youth groups, or dance classes. Unstructured play is vitally important in giving young brains a rest and an opportunity to become more inventive. The essence of creativity comes from play, which feeds and nurtures our souls.

Alarmingly, recess is vanishing in many primary schools. Kindergarteners are expected to acquire "prelearning skills" before they even get to primary school. In Sweden they have a very different approach. There, preschool children are encouraged to play and relax without any structured learning for the first six years of their lives. They go for nature walks every day, even in the bitter Scandinavian winter. They are not taught to read until they are seven years of age, yet by the age of ten, Swedish children consistently lead European literacy rankings.

There is little direct correlation between academic performance and overall success in life, as all sorts of icons have proved. So why do we continue to push our children toward higher and higher test scores? We try to control them in other ways, too. Have you noticed how often you pull on your child's leash instead of giving him or her the freedom to explore? Don't you sometimes get sick of your own voice constantly saying, "No!" or "Don't do that!" or "What are you doing?" or "Where are you going now?" Attempting to direct our children's lives, no matter how good the intention, may prevent them from making mistakes now but also takes away important opportunities for them to learn lessons. Listen to yourself the next time you try to micromanage every move your children make. It is so much more fun to join in with their playfulness and be spontaneously in the moment. And the same goes for micromanaging their education. If a child has a natural talent for tennis but is poor at math, his parents will most likely focus on getting him a math tutor. Sometimes the joy of playing tennis will be denied him so that he can focus on his studies. The irony is that if he wins Wimbledon, he can hire an accountant to figure out his finances.

Success can be measured in many ways, not just in materialistic terms. And success in school isn't just about perfect grades. It is also measured by such attributes as creativity, generosity, and kindness. Having friends and an ability to get along with other people gives children the confidence to find their true purpose. Many of those people who seem to "have it all" will be the first to tell you that they really don't. As my father always said, "Expectation is greater than realization." The words of that armchair philosopher I so dearly miss resonate with me more and more the older I become.

Reflections

Several years ago, I was invited to speak at Fortune's annual conference of the fifty most powerful women in America. After my talk, I offered to lead a mindfulness session. To my surprise, scores of women rushed forward, eager to know how to get calm, reduce stress, and manage their emotions. Most of all, they wanted to learn how to take mindfulness home to their children. A few hours later, I sat on the floor of an impersonal conference room and wondered how many would show up at the designated hour. These were confident, successful people who'd been invited to the conference to share their perspectives and expertise on business, wealth, and the future. I couldn't help but wonder how receptive they would be to mindful meditation. One by one they filed in until the room was crowded. Quietly these besuited women sat cross-legged on the floor, waiting for others, until there was no more room. Clearly there was a thirst for new ways of being, seeing, and functioning in this world. As a brief introduction, I explained what "mindfulness" meant and how our brains need breaks throughout the day. I struck a Tibetan singing bowl, which sent a deep, resonant sound across the room. The whole gathering became still, and I could feel the energy shift as these women followed the sound of the bowl and sank deeper into relaxation. After the power of the silence that we enjoyed together for almost an hour, the women began to open up and share their stories. Many spoke of the difficulties they faced in their corporate world and of parenting at the same time. Several asked how they could continue mindfulness practice within their busy schedules. I suggested that they turn off their phones, ask their assistants to hold their calls, and shut down for ten minutes twice a day. "Sit on your couch or at your desk," I told them. "Listen to silence or put on music that makes you feel good. Focus on your breathing." When the session was over and it was time for the women to move on to the next meeting, several asked if we could do it again. I was overjoyed but realized that the only time we could fit it in was at 5:30 a.m. the following day. I fully expected them to decline, but they jumped at the chance. At dawn the next day, one by one they again entered the room until there was barely space to move.

We face unlimited challenges as parents, so rather than feeling helpless or hopeless, we can learn more positive ways to help shape our brains for greater success and joyfulness.

I hope this knowledge will also help you be more forgiving of yourself as you come to understand the powerful forces constantly at work inside our skulls. Through clarity and focus, we can learn to both understand the mysteries and trust in the power of the mind as well as the heart.

Tuning In to Your Child's Wavelength

*The attentive, caring, and wise voice of a supportive adult
gets internalized and becomes part of the youth's own voice.*

—National Research Council

Loving our children and providing for them are sometimes just not enough. They need our full attention, in which we attune to their feelings so that they feel safe, understood, and connected.

Another term for this is *resonance.* The expression "to be fully present" truly applies with parenting. All this means is that you are giving your children your undivided attention: listening to their every word, picking up on their emotional state, and not thinking of anything beyond their needs in that moment. It is good to be aware of how distracted you really are while talking on the phone, texting, surfing the Internet, or watching TV. While I am not suggesting that we have to drop everything just because the children are clamoring for attention, there are so many distractions these days it is easy for us to lose sight of what's really important and when to make your child a priority over some online gossip site or a television sitcom.

Reflections

"Mommy, Mommy, watch!" A little boy playing baseball in the park repeatedly called to his mother standing a few feet away. She was texting on her cell phone and didn't even look up. He called out again, "Mom!" and again, "Mom!" She never looked up. He eventually turned and walked away. The look on his face broke my heart.

The truth is that whenever you don't pay attention to your children, it hurts them. Just by raising your eyes from your life, you can see what simple pleasure it is that your child is desperate to share. And guess what? These are precious moments you'll never have again.

To find true resonance with your children, consider these four steps:

1. Put aside what you're doing; be fully present and interested. Get down to their level. Offer an open, receptive readiness to see and hear them.

2. Express the proper emotional tone based on the situation, and then accurately reflect their internal experience. If your child comes home with a school project, say something like, "Wow! Did you do that? You must be very proud. How long did it take?"

3. When they express joy at your response, amplify it by reflecting it back with, "That's wonderful, sweetheart. Good job!"

4. If they are sad or frustrated, then honor their feelings and sympathize with them rather than telling them they shouldn't feel that way. These are normal human emotions, and they need to understand that.

Once children feel emotionally secure, they know they are not alone in this world and have someone they can turn to. The important thing is to be vigilant, patient, and consistent so that they are assured that they can come to you in times of crisis as well as joy. Every day you can ask yourself, "Have I helped my children understand their gifts and talents? Did I empathize with their feelings enough? Is there something I can do or say now to help strengthen our connection?"

Attuning like this isn't always easy for us to do, particularly when our children have chosen not to share their true feelings with us. Sometimes they may appear to be crying over something like a lost toy when, in fact, their tears are actually a symptom of what they are feeling about something else. Does the toy represent a parent missed from a broken home? Or are they just cranky because they didn't get enough sleep?

Mindful parenting involves recognizing and nurturing our children's unique personalities and not seeing them as projec-

> *If the child's primary caretaker is available and responsive . . . then the child develops a foundation of faith that key people in her life will be available and supportive when she needs them.*
>
> —Sharon Begley

tions of ourselves. There's simply no cookie-cutter standard for
how we treat our children; they
need us to see and support their
individuality. But only when we
have clear vision of our own lives
can we support our children fully
in becoming the best of who
they are.

> *When we put our children aside
> while we do something else and
> rely on objects to hold them and
> entertain them, we are encourag-
> ing them to be passive, powerless
> recipients in a loving, responsive
> world.*
>
> —Jon Kabat-Zinn, PhD

Reflections

When I was twelve, egged on by a girlfriend and feeling a
level of peer pressure, I did the unthinkable. I stole a hot pink
skirt from a neighborhood store. It was the first and last time
I ever did such a thing. Arriving home, I was so frightened, I
was shaking. What had I done? I remember walking to the
back room where my mom was sitting by the fire. She looked
at me askew. "What a pretty skirt," she said. Trembling, I
told her I'd just bought it for a dollar. She shot me a dark look
and said nothing. I knew she didn't believe me. I quivered a
smile and slowly turned and went upstairs. Sitting alone in my
room, I began to cry and cry and cry. I felt so guilty. I finally
burst out of my room and, running to the top of the stairs,
wailed, "Mom!" In her deep gravelly voice, she said, "Yes,
Goldie?" I sobbed, "I stole that skirt." There was a pause and
then she said, "I know you did. Now come down here. Let's
talk about this." She sat me down and asked me why I did it.
I told her that I didn't know. I was confused and my girlfriend

made me do it. My mother took me into the store to pay for the skirt and then hung it on the back of my bedroom door for one year. Neither of us took it down in that time. That pretty much did it for me where pink is concerned—you won't catch me in that color. I couldn't fool my mother; she was so attuned to me, she knew me better than anybody. She knew I was lying, she knew I needed to stew in my guilt until I confessed, and lovingly she knew how to skillfully teach me a lesson I'd never forget.

Self-awareness is everything when it comes to really tuning in to our children. We need to be fully aware of what we are doing that might prevent us from finding a resonance with them, and that includes our own life experiences and how they make us react. Whenever we become mindful of not making the mistakes our parents made, chances are that we'll think before we act. By dealing with our own issues through awareness, we can shift perspective and do some brain pruning of our own, replacing a negative with a positive outlook. Here's what we need to do:

- Pay attention

- Break the chain of negative imprints

- Avoid passing on a negative legacy

If you're a single parent, here's the good news: according to research, children only need one strong relationship with a primary caregiver in order to create a sense of self and healthy, long-lasting relationships with others.

In one study of teenage children, researchers found that race, income, or a specific family structure did not predict risk-taking behavior such as drug or alcohol abuse, driving too fast, or taking chances in games. What protected children most from dangerous behavior was a strong relationship with at least one adult. So if we are single parents (as I have been), we can take comfort in the knowledge that we can be enough.

> Parents are the active sculptors of their children's growing brains. The immature brain of the child is so sensitive to social experience that adoptive parents should in fact also be called biological parents because the family experiences they create shape the biological structure of their child's brain.
>
> —Daniel J. Siegel, MD

Neuroscientists estimate that 50 percent of happiness is an inherited predisposition, leaving 50 percent in our control. This is something we can actively help nurture, no matter if we are alone or part of a couple.

MANAGING OUR REACTIONS

The joy of parenting can make our hearts fuller than we ever thought possible. There are so many moments to be savored. The challenges of parenting can also fill our heads with emotions other than happiness. There are so many times when our children drive us crazy and make us want to tear our hair out. Parenting is an odyssey of sorts, an adventure fraught with daily challenges but illuminated with countless wonders.

But when we feel overwhelmed or strained to the breaking point, how do we manage our own anger, frustration, and fear?

How do we find a place of inner calm so that we can see more clearly what's really happening with and to our children, uncolored by overpowering emotions? At times it seems the simple solution is to avoid confrontation and get over the rough patches relatively unscathed.

> When we practice mindful awareness, we come to understand more about our minds. We recognize that our thoughts and feelings come and go, ebb and tide. This awareness helps us manage our emotions better.
>
> —Daniel Goleman, PhD

Self-denial is a very strong human instinct, especially during challenging times. It takes a lot of courage to face our fears and to admit our own failings. The good news is that how we react can be controlled by being more conscious of our thoughts. We can engage our own prefrontal cortex—the Wise Old Owl of the brain, where our higher and more critical thinking occurs—just as we hope our children will learn to do. In order for us to be our best selves, we must bravely examine our feelings and actions and admit the truth about our own behavior. I call it "standing on watch," which is not an easy task.

Reactive parenting can be very detrimental for our children. Yelling at them for forgetting something or doing something we don't like only frightens them—it doesn't make them stop. We can gain control over our anger by understanding that our higher thinking has been hijacked by our emotional state; hence, we're no longer in control.

EMOTIONALLY HIJACKED

The anger and frustration that we feel in such moments is simply our Guard Dog amygdala responding to the perceived stressful situation and taking over our emotions. Once we understand this, we can learn to recognize when we've been hijacked and accept that the path back to clear thinking is mindful awareness. Simply being in a state of awareness automatically stimulates the neurotransmitters that calm down the amygdala and light up the prefrontal cortex.

> If I have my eyes closed and sit silently for a while, it is cool. It's very relaxing. It calms you down when you go crazy or wacko.
>
> —Lisa, age 11

It sounds almost an oversimplification, but try it—it works. In soothing our minds, we can reduce cortisol levels, increase dopamine, and reflect on what may have triggered our emotional reaction in the first place. We can retrain our brains to be less reactive when we observe what happened and make more mindful choices next time.

Even when we are hijacked and respond inappropriately, it isn't the end of the world. There are ways to repair the damage done. According to John Gottman, author of *Raising an Emotionally Intelligent Child*, we should never be embarrassed to admit our mistakes, for when we do, our children will feel free to come to us when they make mistakes. He suggests we do the following:

■ **Calm down:** Don't do anything until your amygdala is off guard duty and your prefrontal cortex is functioning again.

- **Apologize:** Tell your child, "I got hijacked and lost my mind. I'm sorry. It's back now."

- **Reestablish connection:** With young ones, you can console and hug, or have them draw or write about how they feel. With older ones, you can discuss both your roles in what happened.

By helping our children understand exactly what's going on inside their brains when they are upset—or when we are—they'll be able to see situations more logically. And by using certain techniques outlined in the following chapters, they can learn to take control and ultimately to recognize and reduce their own stress.

Even when we understand the reasons behind our negative reactions and poor behavior, it doesn't mean the end of conflict. Conflict is a normal and healthy part of family life. It's okay to be angry every now and again. In fact, according to research, parent-child conflict can even promote mental growth and moral development if we learn how to control it. Just as stress can either energize us or overwhelm us, conflict can either spark us to thoughtfulness and action or set off a conflagration. The choice is always ours.

> *Every brain system we know about, whether it relates to the visual, the auditory system, or language, is shaped by experience.*
>
> —Helen Neville, PhD

Our children are facing challenges never experienced by any previous generation. In an overstimulating, fast-paced society, they are at tremendous emotional risk—whether it's from the breakdown of the family, the collapse of our economic system, or the pressure to succeed. By helping them help themselves, we can help them handle their stress and, in so doing, remind ourselves of the importance of managing our own.

Reflections

There was a point in my life at the busiest time of my career when I felt overwhelmed by responsibilities—and sadness. My marriage was falling apart, and I keenly felt the loss of family and the fracturing of a dream. This was not what I wanted. I knew I needed help, so I went to see a psychiatrist. He listened to me complain about how swamped I felt by work and taking care of my sick mother and my children. Then he said something that changed the way I thought about my life: "Who told you that you were some kind of goddess who could do everything? Is that who you think you are?" He made me realize that I had developed an inflated view of myself, believing that I could—and should—do it all. It came as such a relief to be given permission not to be perfect, to admit that I was human and flawed. All I had to do was say no. My choices became much clearer, and I was no longer driven by what was expected of me. I chose not to attend breakfast meetings or business dinners if they took me away from my kids. It didn't make sense for me to be out "saving the world" at dozens of charitable events for children if it meant leaving my own children. I came to realize that the world wouldn't fall apart if I removed myself from it. Saying no was so liberating; it freed me to be completely present with my children.

Talking with Your Child About the Brain

I am better at writing. I am persistent. I am calm. I have perspective to be still and be a friend. I am happy. It helps me be healthy. I am smart. It helps me read.

—Melissa, age 10

For children, finding out about their brains can be astonishing and liberating—a true "lightbulb" moment. Mindful awareness of what is happening in their day-to-day lives—and how they respond—strengthens their self-control. Engaging the powers of the prefrontal cortex heightens their attention and enhances their ability to attune to themselves and the world around them. In turn, this increases their capacity for empathy, a vital quality for helping them cope with work, school, and relationships. Focused and calm, they can be less stressed, more receptive, and emotionally and mentally fitter.

The practical applications of having such knowledge are infinite, and are best demonstrated in how children manage their reactions to events and other people, especially when they are feeling anger, fear, and stress. Knowing that the amygdala not only *detects* fear but *generates* it can make all the difference.

With this information, children can also begin to understand what triggers the hijacking of their emotions and how it is different for everyone. It all depends on what the brain decides is threatening based on each person's past experience.

THE WORKINGS OF THE BRAIN AND HOW TO EXPLAIN THEM

Learning about how the brain works should be as fun as it is educational for you and your children. Choosing the right time to get started is important because you don't want to give your children the impression that they are back in the classroom. It is always best to make any discussion a natural part of your daily interactions. Times when you can be thoughtful and distractions are at a minimum include when you're sitting down to dinner together, at bedtime, or when you're just out for a walk. While it's not uncommon for you to ask your children what they learned at school that day, you may find that you get their attention by telling them a personal story that will lead into the discussion of how the brain works. If, for example, you were thinking about something that happened and your own reaction to it, your experience provides an easy introduction to the workings of the brain, whether it was a scare that triggered your fight-or-flight response or, on the more positive side, how you felt when you helped an older person with her groceries.

Sometimes the right time presents itself in the middle of an emotional crisis or stressful situation. It could be during a fight with a sibling, before a school test, after a particularly tough day at school, or following just a plain old tantrum triggered by some seemingly inconsequential incident. Your first instinct is to comfort your child. Any discussion you might want to have usually starts with taking a few deep breaths together so that you can both become calmer and more receptive. This is the ideal opportunity to explain briefly why deep breathing helps us, because you'll both be experiencing the positive effects of this simple exercise immediately.

With everyone in a quieter state of mind, you can talk about how the brain has a habit of taking over and causing all kinds of trouble unless we learn to understand what's going on and to control how we respond. You want your children to appreciate that they can choose to be happy rather than sad and miserable. However you find your way into the subject, you will want to share the wonders of the brain and your own sense of discovery with your children. Once they find out what the brain does and how it works, they'll be amazed, too. Keep it fun and playful. Remember: a happy child is more eager to learn.

In the following section, I have tried to translate the information from the first few chapters into child-friendly language, providing some guidance gleaned from teachers and researchers working with the MindUP program. The scripts are only suggestions to follow. You can adapt these discussions to his or her age, understanding, and attention span. And though it is impossible to anticipate every question your child may have, I've included a "Frequently Asked Questions" list at the end of this brief teaching section.

Depending on your child's age, he or she may know more about the brain than you think. Regardless, you will probably want to be prepared with some visual aids that show the parts of the brain. You can do simple drawings together. (Even if you aren't artistically inclined, your child will appreciate your efforts, and the time you spend together will be much more personal and feel less like a lecture and more like a game.) You can also find lots of good illustrations on the Internet. You may even wish to use the computer to help illustrate your points, but don't let the computer become a substitute teacher.

TALKING THE TALK

"Your brain," you can tell your child, "is like all the stuff that's under the hood of a car—the engine and all the electrical parts that make everything work. Without the engine, the car won't move, the lights won't work, the steering wheel won't turn, and the radio won't play. Without your brain, you couldn't see, hear, feel, talk, run, or do anything—it's a really important part of you. But your brain isn't made of metal and wires, just like your body isn't made of glass, steel, and rubber like a car.

"Your brain is round with lots of bumps and wrinkles, sort of like a big walnut only much softer. That's why it's protected by your skull—like the helmet you wear when you go biking. It's about the size of two of your fists when you hold them together. And like the two fists, the brain is divided into two halves, called *hemispheres*.

"Like the engine of a car, different parts of the brain are

responsible for different things. One part, called the *reptilian brain*, takes care of all the stuff you do without having to think about it, like making your heart beat or your lungs breathe or your throat swallow your food.

"Another part, the *limbic* or *emotional brain*, is responsible for the way you feel—like being happy or sad or worried. An important bit of the limbic brain is the *amygdala*; that's a funny word to describe something that is like a Guard Dog that barks when it senses that something bad—or sometimes something good—is happening. So if you see something scary, the amygdala might send out a signal to your body to fight the bad guy. Or to run away. Or to stay really still and not move, like a frightened bunny. It's called fight, flight, or freeze. Sometimes things happen that make us angry or afraid. The problem is that the amygdala can make us feel like we're in danger when we're really not.

"Or our Guard Dog might sense something pleasant and send out a signal to smile and be happy, like when you see your best friend coming down the sidewalk.

"And then there's the biggest part, the *cortical brain*. That's the part that looks like a big walnut. It's responsible for remembering and thinking about stuff, talking, and helping you pay attention. The front of the cortical brain, just behind your forehead, is the *prefrontal cortex*. This is what we might call the Wise Old Owl of the brain that looks at stuff, thinks about it, and remembers what you see and hear. It's in charge of thinking, planning, reasoning, solving problems, making good choices about what you do. It also helps make sure that you don't let your emotions take over and do mean things because you're sad or angry."

Once you have talked about the parts of the brain, you can reinforce the ideas by recounting the story you told about yourself at the beginning. This time, you can explain that it was your amygdala—your inner Guard Dog—that went into action and helped you respond to a situation. And, of course, getting your child to think of a time when his amygdala really helped him, and to describe how he felt, will make this lesson come alive.

Ask, "Can you think of a time when your amygdala *didn't* help you?"

Guide your child with a story about something that happened on the playground or when she got into a silly fight. Remind her that sometimes the Guard Dog helps us and saves us from danger but that sometimes it stops us from thinking straight and making good decisions.

Make a list together of some of the sensations your child might feel when her amygdala starts "barking":

- Sweating or shaking

- Pounding heart

- Feeling a tummyache or thinking she might throw up

- Breathing faster

- Feeling the urge to cry

Ask your child how she thinks she might be able to calm herself down in such a situation. And, at this point, you can introduce the idea of mindful breathing simply by suggesting that taking the time to breathe deeply and count to ten before doing anything will help—and that the Guard Dog will stop barking, calm down, and go back into his kennel. Explain that once she has gotten it under control, her brain will relax and the Wise Old

Owl will help her think clearly again. Remind her that whenever she gets upset in the future, all she has to do is breathe and sit quietly and everything will feel better.

Once you've covered the basics, be patient with your child—and yourself. Learning doesn't happen overnight. Keep at it and follow up on it whenever the time feels right. Have some fun. When your child comes home from school, ask, "How was your day? Did your Guard Dog get overexcited today? Did the Wise Old Owl help you at all?" You might get some interesting answers.

> *Children come to see their own minds in a new light and realize that their minds matter. This makes a difference to how they'll learn. It reinforces the enjoyment and impact of the experience of learning.*
>
> —Daniel J. Siegel, MD

Once children grasp the basics, you'll be having very different conversations throughout your years of parenting. Your children will be able to put their emotions in context by using visual images of Wise Old Owls and Guard Dogs to help them understand exactly what is going on inside their heads.

Frequently Asked Questions

- What is the name of the structure that acts like a Guard Dog? (*the amygdala*)
- When the hair on our neck stands up and we feel like running away, what is this an example of? (*flight*)
- What part of our brain is located immediately behind the forehead and acts like a Wise Old Owl? (*the prefrontal cortex*)
- When someone pushes us in the playground, this is an example of what? (*fight*)
- Which part of our brain helps protect us from danger? (*the amygdala*)
- Which part of our brain helps us make good choices? (*the prefrontal cortex*)
- When we lash out at someone else or use angry words without thinking, what part of our brain is that coming from? (*the amygdala*)

7

Mindful Breathing

*The breath is simply a means of befriending this deep capacity
of the heart and mind. . . . Without judging, condemning or
forcing, come back to this moment, this breath; each breath a
new beginning; each out breath a letting go; no agenda; just
this moment, this breath, outside of time; timeless.*

—Jon Kabat-Zinn, PhD

We human beings are an amazing species. As far as we know,
we're the only animal on the planet that can watch our own
minds and actions in a self-analyzing way that can lead to a
change of direction. This ability is called *metacognition.*

Fortunately, there is a simple way to turn on this ability that
takes no money or special equipment and has all kinds of beneficial effects. It is called *mindful breathing.*

Instinctively, we all know the benefit of taking a few deep
breaths before or during a stressful moment. How many times
have we said to ourselves, "Stop, take a breath," as we feel it center us. Ever present, ever available, our breath is something we
can tune in to anytime we want and use as a kind of gentle met-
ronome to set the pace of our awareness practices. Mindful

breathing is one of the best ways of practicing *mindful awareness* because our breath brings oxygen to our brains and bodies, creating a sense of calm.

There are many interpretations of the word "mindfulness." Its most common interpretation involves the use of meditation. But mindfulness includes many other aspects. One is contemplation. Being mindfully aware may sound difficult at first, but it's not. Nor is it something we have to work hard to achieve. Mindful awareness is simply paying attention to what is happening now. In doing nothing other than living in the moment for a few minutes, we can let thoughts and feelings come and go without holding on to them or judging them. In doing so, we build the muscles of concentration, observation, and relaxation all at the same time.

This is different from thinking, in which we often judge each moment on what has been or what could be. I sometimes call it *mind-full* awareness because the mind is full of nothing but a gentle focus on the breath. It is the direct opposite to being *mind-less*. Mindlessness is when we are on autopilot and not paying attention to the present moment. We've all been there. We sometimes feel as though we are sleepwalking through our lives. Minutes, hours, even days can go by that we don't fully recall because we don't feel aware of what is happening.

> By sitting and mindfully breathing for ten minutes a day, in as little as eight weeks you strengthen the part of the prefrontal cortex involved in generating positive feelings and diminish the part that generates negative ones.
>
> —Richard Davidson, PhD

Sometimes in mindlessness we find ourselves reacting automatically in negative ways—lashing out or saying things we later regret. We ask ourselves, "Why did I do that?" or "Who was in charge of my mouth?" It doesn't have to be this way. We all have the ability to become more present. First we have to truly believe it is possible. Then we create the intention. The more we tune in to our own thoughts and feelings, the more choices we give ourselves in terms of our responses.

The key to all these mindful practices is to keep going and not be overcritical of ourselves. Whenever we become aware that our minds have wandered from our practice, we just gently refocus. Learning expert Tim Gallwey calls this "awareness without judgment" and claims that it is one of the greatest tools for learning in what he describes as the "inner game." The more we reinforce this message, the more we improve our own focus—and the more we help our children accept that they can make mistakes without being overcritical of themselves.

The benefits of mindful breathing have been recognized for centuries and across all cultures, but in recent times they have been especially helpful for those in high-stress jobs. The practice is taught to everyone from Olympic athletes to firefighters. In a program called Mindfulness-based Mind Fitness Training, or "M-fit," U.S. military personnel learn mindful breathing as part of stress resilience against the extreme experi-

> One little girl was having a hard time adjusting to kindergarten, so we dropped her to half a day, but that didn't help. Her reaction was so severe that we wondered if she should stay in school. Then I decided to take her into my office a few times a day to practice mindful breathing, and she began to improve. After three weeks of us doing no other intervention except breathing with her a few times a day, she was able to stay in school all day long.
>
> —Elizabeth Z., primary school teacher

ences in war zones. Similar techniques are taught to emergency responders, law enforcement officers, care providers, crisis workers, and intelligence analysts.

In one landmark study, Jon Kabat-Zinn, PhD, took two groups of healthy people and taught one group mindful awareness practices, in which they focused mainly on their breathing. After three months, the mindful awareness group showed a 44 percent decrease in psychological distress, a 46 percent decrease in illnesses such as colds and headaches, and a 24 percent decrease in the stress response to everyday challenges. The other group showed no changes. Here are just some of the powerful effects of mindful breathing and awareness discovered in over a thousand studies:

- Calms the stress response

- Strengthens attention

- Promotes brain integration

- Fosters better sleep

- Strengthens self-awareness

Reflections

I remember the first day I tried mindful breathing. I purposefully chose a room that would be free of distractions: a simple straight-back chair, a small table with a vase holding a single rose, and a burning stick of incense. I sat down, closed my eyes, and tried to recall what I'd been instructed to do. It felt strange at first. I noticed my breathing was not regular; my mind thought about that, but then I remembered that I was supposed to let go of those thoughts and went back to focusing on my breath. A warm breeze blew through an open window, and I felt it and attended to the sensation, but then I went back to my breathing. I felt my entire body relax piece by piece. I felt my arms relax, my legs relax, my stomach relax. For the first time in months, I began to unwind. Suddenly something happened. I felt as light as a feather. I honestly felt as if I were meeting my true self again after a long time. It was as if I were reconnecting with an old friend who'd been abandoned in all the hustle of everyday struggles and life. I wanted to laugh. I felt so full of joy that I let myself giggle out loud. I was amazed at how such a simple exercise could yield such benefits. Sitting there laughing at myself, with myself, was so uplifting and liberating. It was an experience that I will never forget as long as I live.

MINDFUL
BREATHING
PRACTICE

Although you can do mindful breathing anywhere—in the car, on a train, even in a restroom—it's sometimes helpful to create a special space to do it in. It doesn't have to be large, just a corner of a room where there's a comfortable place to sit. It's a great idea for both you and your family to have a space where anyone can go when they need to take a "brain break."

Many mindful practitioners use a bell or chime to begin and end their breathing practice. It's not necessary, but you may find that works for you, too. It doesn't matter what the instrument is—

> Your children's breathing is the swinging door between their inner and outer worlds.
>
> —Susan Kaiser Greenland, PhD

it can be a length of copper pipe hit with a fork—it just has to have a resonance to its sound that floats on the air long after it has been struck. Listen to the note that lingers. Hear its tone and then inhabit the empty space that follows.

The process of mindful breathing is very simple. All you do is focus on your breathing. As one breath ends, so the next begins. Many of us breathe very shallowly, with only the upper portion of our lungs. This is particularly true whenever we are hunched over a computer or on a cell phone. The more stressed and excited we become, the shallower we breathe. Filling our lungs from the bottom up energizes our body. The outgoing breath relaxes the body.

Your eyes do not have to be closed, but your mind should be very much in the present. Soften your belly. Breathe slowly in and then let the air out. Your mind will undoubtedly wander because that's what the brain does naturally; it thinks night and day, providing a running faucet of thoughts. (Some people call this "monkey chatter.") Whether you like it or not, your mind will offer up endless commentary.

Don't be hard on yourself. Each time you notice that you have wandered off into thoughts, feelings, or sensations, let them go; don't attach to them. See these thoughts as clouds floating across the sky of your mind; then just allow them to drift away. Let your focus gently settle instead on the vast blue expanse of sky, not on the clouds flitting by. Then gently bring your attention back to your breath. The more frequently you practice, the easier it will become, because it's the noticing that your mind has wandered off and bringing it back that builds the mental muscle.

When it comes to teaching mindful breathing to your children, ask them to sit comfortably with their hands in their laps and close their eyes. If they are not comfortable closing their eyes, they can focus on a single object, such as a picture, a window, or their hands. Start with a few seconds sitting still and breathing at first, and gradually build up to a few minutes. Young children will often only sit still for a minute or two at a time. Older children will be able to go a little longer, maybe ten minutes at a time. Slowly stretch out the time spent sitting in silence.

> *Sometimes when I'm fighting with my friends, I walk away and just breathe for a while because I don't want to make them mad at me because then we won't be friends anymore.*
>
> —Kevin, age 9

Tell the children to feel the rise and fall of their bellies as they breathe. Ask them to put their hands on their bellies to feel the movement. This is a great technique to help them focus and make sure they are breathing deeply enough. Explain that when we take quick, shallow breaths we become tense, and when we take slow, deep breaths we relax. With older children, you can remind them that deep breathing calms the amygdala and that they can use this to focus better whenever they need to.

Be prepared for distractions once you have settled down together and are breathing. The noises of everyday life will interrupt, such as a dog barking, a telephone ringing, or a car passing by. Your children may start to fidget, which is perfectly normal.

If that happens, just encourage them to bring their attention back each time to their breath. The calmer and softer you are in giving instructions, the more peaceful the experience will be. The more often you do this together, the less need there will be for instruction.

With practice, you can build up to breathing mindfully a couple of times a day for maybe five minutes at a time. Then later you can do it more often and for longer. Your experience should be deeply personal.

After each practice, share with your children what it felt like. Talk about the ways in which mindful breathing could be used—maybe when they are being bothered by a friend or are nervous about a game. From now on, before you begin any of the activities in this book (with or without your children), practice a few minutes of mindful breathing first. The more you practice, the more you'll feel the benefits until it becomes completely natural. And once it does, you'll become aware of how positively this affects and informs your day.

In a world that demands instant gratification, we often expect instant results. With some of these practices we have to be patient, and we will find them easier to do on some days than others. That's normal. Hang in there.

If you think this is going to take too much time out of your day, then think again. All that is needed to create change is *three minutes* of mindful breathing a day, according to a recent study in the *Proceedings of the National Academy of Sciences*. What strengthens the brain is not the length of time that we do the practice but the frequency with which we practice during a day. For example, sitting for twenty minutes doing mindful breathing is not as effective as doing it three times a day for three minutes each time. (And, frankly, it is a lot easier, especially when you are just starting out.)

Not only do mindfulness practices make us feel better in the moment, through the release of feel-good hormones such as dopamine and serotonin, but the effects are cumulative and lasting as well. Thanks to the miracle of brain plasticity, these effects create enduring differences in our brains. So every time we stop and quiet our minds, we're building healthier habits of thinking and feeling. The more we practice, the more these behaviors become automatic in ourselves and our kids. Eventually, we and our children will become more reflective than reactive, with stronger brain circuitry for self-awareness, emotional control, and attention. Remember, practice makes permanent.

> *Think of mindful breathing as creating prefrontal reinforcements for challenging times in the future. . . . Mindful awareness feels so good because it uses the same brain circuitry that's activated when we emotionally attune to someone else.*
>
> —Daniel J. Siegel, MD

Reflections

It was Christmas Eve, and we were at our ranch in Colorado. It was snowing hard outside, and family and friends were inside helping to decorate the tree. There were more grown-ups than children—about fifteen of us in all, excited and chatting, happy to be together and looking forward to yet another annual tradition. It was almost the time of the evening when one of us was to read the poem "The Night Before Christmas" by Clement C. Moore. My grandson Ryder, who was four years old, had chosen Kurt (known as "Go-Gi") to read it that year. The room was noisy and animated, and no one would settle down. I tried to yell above the din that it was time: "Santa's coming soon, so after the poem, all the children have to go to bed." Ryder tugged at my sleeve. "Go-Go," he said, using the name my grandchildren use for me. I bent down and he whispered in my ear, "Can we do some breathing together first?" You could have knocked me over with a feather. Although I knew he'd been taught mindful breathing in preschool, I couldn't believe that my grandson had the presence of mind at such a young age to know how to settle down the troops. With his help we made a circle, and I asked Ryder to lead us in our breathing. Sure enough, he gave everyone instructions, and for the next three minutes the room was quiet except for the crackling of the log fire. Within seconds a great soft blanket of peace fell over our Christmas Eve thanks to a four-year-old boy. He created the space for us to focus on being together and share that most magical of nights. We really heard every word of the poem as Kurt began to read: "'Twas the night before Christmas, when all through the house, not a creature was stirring, not even a mouse. . . ." By reminding us of the importance of reflection, the youngest among us had helped us to cherish the blessings that we had.

PRACTICE WHAT
WE PREACH

Mindful breathing is probably the single most important practice in this book because it can be used to help with all the other practices and applied to hundreds of situations within an ordinary day. I call it the "secret sauce."

> My dad was helping me build a model airplane and it fell apart. He was so mad. He was saying bad words. I told him, "Dad, why don't you sit down and just breathe for a while and relax? It's only a model."
>
> —Chad, age 8

Money, work, children, or health issues are all normal concerns that can sometimes overwhelm us. Mindful breathing is a life preserver, especially for parents whose children are coping with severe challenges. The ability to bring ourselves back to a neutral position that will give us the focus and muscle we need to help manage our complex emotions is vital. Children afraid of anything from monsters in the cupboard to our planet in peril can draw on their mindful breathing to similarly neutralize their anxieties. Angry children can discover ways to manage their temper. Hyperactive children can use mindful breathing as a tool to quiet down and gain awareness of their own hyperactivity. A teenager who expresses frustration and disappointment can learn to focus on the moment, reduce his stress, and give himself more perspective.

Sleep

Mindful breathing helps me go to sleep. It helps me think, and it helps me concentrate. —SOPHIE, AGE 9

One of the great discoveries in our research for the MindUP program was that mindful breathing also helped children sleep better. Lack of sleep has been linked to a wide range of physical and psychological issues, including obesity, Type 2 diabetes, depression, and behavioral problems.

Scientists now believe that while stress can cause insomnia, lack of sleep can also cause stress. We all know the feeling: after a couple of restless nights we feel irritable, angry, and unable to cope. Our skin tone changes, and our eyes become ringed with dark circles. The cycle continues. The next night we become stressed that yet more hours of sleeplessness await us.

Mindful breathing helps adults go to sleep faster, sleep better and longer, and wake up less in the night.

—DR. RAMADEVI GOURINENI

Sadly, the same goes for our children. Suffering the same symptoms that we do is bad enough, but then they are expected to go to school and learn.

While children sleep, their brains preserve relevant memories from the day that can help them learn in the future. Sleep is so vital to our overall well-being that we need to do everything we can to ensure the whole family is getting enough.

The U.S. Centers for Disease Control and Prevention offers a guide for how much sleep we should be getting for optimum physical, emotional, and mental health:

- Adults need at least 7 hours of sleep every night.
- Adolescents need at least 8.5 hours.
- Five- to twelve-year-olds need at least 9 hours.
- Three- to five-year-olds need at least 11 hours.

A wonderful way to prepare ourselves for a good night's sleep is with mindful breathing. By calming the mind and focusing on the breath, we can reduce our heart rate and relax our body.

One dramatic example of how it can help came from a young boy who'd been unable to sleep through the night for two years because he was being bullied. He begged to stay home from school and was suffering academically. After learning mindful breathing, he slept through the night for the first time and soon began to enjoy going to school again. "If I do wake up anxious," he told his teachers, "I just do my mindful breathing and then I fall asleep."

Reflections

I was trained as a ballet dancer, and all I wanted to be when I grew up was a dance teacher. Whenever we'd finish our routine, our choreographer would say, "Okay, everybody, let's go back to Position One." When I first learned to breathe with awareness, I realized that this is what mindful awareness is—Position One for our mind, body, and spirit after the busy routines of life. Ever since that realization, I make sure I have my quiet time every day. Even when my children were small and would follow me everywhere, I'd try to find time for my breathing when they were napping or make it the last thing I did at night (which always made me sleep long and deeply). As my children got older, I'd tell them, "Mommy's going to quiet her mind now." They'd tease me about going to "stare at a wall." Another way we speak of it in our family is in terms of "turning our eyes on ourselves." Whenever I get quiet—and especially at night—I turn my eyeballs back to me. Safe inside myself and breathing deeply, I've learned to witness the good and the bad without judgment, helping me achieve clearer vision. You really can stop the frenzy just by getting quiet and focusing on the breath. You can't imagine the peace and the joy that you'll feel in just a few minutes. Try it. It's helped me in all the ways I've described, but best of all, I drift off to sleep peacefully and surrender fearlessly.

Mindful Sensing

*Children are born true scientists. They spontaneously
experiment and experience and re-experience again. . . .
They smell, taste, bite, and touch-test for hardness, softness,
springiness, roughness, smoothness, coldness, warmness.*

—R. Buckminster Fuller

Mindful sensing is about taking the time to really pay attention to the remarkable sensation of being alive, moment to moment, in our bodies. In other words, it's appreciating all that we see, hear, smell, taste, and feel. This may seem obvious, but it's not that easy.

We are always telling our children to *pay attention*, but if we are finding it increasingly difficult to focus, then how can we expect them to do it? Children have just as many distractions around them as we do but not as much experience in how to manage them. And we now know from neural experts and psychologists that these daily diversions actually rewire the brain's capacity to concentrate.

Mindful sensing is another great way to interrupt the constant static of the modern age. It is important for us and our children to know that we can focus if we just learn to center our-selves and become fully aware of the sensations around us.

Reflections

When my children were little, I would take them on hikes along the beach or in the woods to search for rocks in the shape of hearts, because the heart is one of my favorite sym-bols. As a family, we had so many memorable outings, keep-ing our heads down, focusing on every little pebble in our quest, and then sharing what we'd discovered. It was great fun, but little did I know then how meaningful an activity it was—how healthy it was for my children's young brains to remain focused on something so natural for several minutes at a time. I still have some of the heart rocks my children and I found, and just recently my son Wyatt brought me another that he found on the seashore in Germany during a day off between hockey games. I was thrilled, both that he remem-bered my love for heart stones and that he still knew the im-portance of quiet, reflective time between moments of stress.

Every second of every day our brains are inundated with bil-lions of pieces of sensory data coming at us from all sides. Ninety-nine percent of this information is discarded almost instantly upon entering our brains, according to psychology professor Mi-chael Gazzaniga of the University of California. Think of it as water draining through a sieve.

If we paid attention to everything, our brains would soon

become overloaded, so we register only the most important pieces of information. Sitting in a room close to a ticking clock as we read a book, for example, we might also hear the sound of a distant car or smell a meal cooking in the oven. We might notice the sensation of being too warm or glance up to see a bird preening itself on a branch outside the window. We'd feel a sensation on our leg when the pet dog rubs up against us or notice a dryness in our mouths informing us that we're thirsty. This ability to discern between sensory data comes from a specialized part of our brain that unconsciously filters what we should pay attention to, when, and why.

Once we begin to practice focusing through mindful awareness, we can develop more conscious control of what we pay attention to. This is because we grow stronger neural pathways in our brain. In other words, rather than becoming lost in the electronic data forest, we become better at seeing individual trees. Not only that, but we acquire the capacity to choose *which* tree to pay attention to, because all other sensory data coming at us get filtered out or toned down to insignificance. The ability to focus is a crucial skill for success in life.

Neuroscientists have discovered several critical networks in the prefrontal cortex that enable us to concentrate, evaluate information, and make decisions. This area also helps us recognize our emotional state and decide how to respond. More interestingly, perhaps, scientists have found that these networks overlap. Mindful sensing practices not only strengthen the neural networks for focus but simultaneously activate and strengthen those controlling emotional balance and the highest operations of executive function.

If we could see inside our brains while we're doing something as simple as looking for a heart-shaped stone, we'd see specific areas light up. We'd also notice that the circuitries for decision making and emotional regulation light up at the same time. So although mindful sensing may seem like a frivolous activity or a distraction from learning, nothing could be further from the truth. How amazing is that?

> It is the senses that are the only way to feel the world. The mind itself is a sense . . . you can see without seeing, you can hear all sorts of things and not hear.
>
> —Jon Kabat-Zinn, PhD

MINDFUL LISTENING

How many times a week do we misunderstand what someone has said? How often have we witnessed a conversation in which one person cuts off the other before the first has finished expressing her thoughts? Mindful listening reinforces a crucial skill of emotional intelligence: the ability to listen accurately to others with our minds and hearts without interrupting or leaping to conclusions.

We especially need to listen to what our children have to say. They'll tell us everything if we just attend to them, so we need to perfect the art of being quiet. Whenever we practice mindful listening, we strengthen awareness and refine the ability to really hear. Feeling as if you are not being heard is one of the most hurtful things in any relationship. In focusing on the words being spoken, we're able to fully pay attention. We are also able to absorb what someone is saying before making judgments based on the past or projections into the future.

Strengthening such awareness helps our children to be less

reactive, too. By listening mindfully, they'll become aware of the gifts of language and understand the differences in intonation.

Lisa Aziz-Zadeh, assistant professor of occupational sciences at the University of Southern California, scanned the brains of young volunteers as they heard and repeated a nonsensical phrase intoned in several different ways. She found that the higher a person scored in empathy tests, the more activity he or she had in the areas of the brain that produce and process the sounds of speech. This research helps us to understand that not only is listening important for absorbing information but it also stimulates our ability to feel empathy for others, creating a more caring and attuned human being.

> *After we did mindful listening practice, I was at home on the computer and my mom was talking to me, and I realized that I wasn't listening. I shut down the lid and asked her to say it again so that I could pay attention.*
>
> —Clark, age 10

With every new gadget and technological fad, we are adding more and more layers of sound to our world, turning on and tuning out. We are losing our silence.

George Prochnik, author of *In Pursuit of Silence: Listening for Meaning in a World of Noise*, warns that the disappearance of silent spaces is endangering our ability to obtain a reflective, active state of mind. "The quest always begins in silence," he says, "whether it's an animal stalking its prey or a thinker answering a question. The start of the question is silence." New York writer J. Gabriel Boylan summarizes the dangers of our constant exposure to noise: "The peak of brain activity, of thinking, comes in the tiny pauses between sounds, when we simultaneously process the previous sound and anticipate the next. When noise never abates, brain activity tends to flatline." In other words, living with constant noise dulls your brain.

The following practices will help strengthen listening abilities. Some will feed our natural instinct for silence. Some involve music, which can, believe it or not, improve learning and memory. New research has proved that music can be more than just an enhancement; it may actually change the shape of the brain. This is because the nerves in the ear have more brain connections than any other nerves in the body. They affect the glands, the nervous system, blood pressure, and mental awareness. Children who learn to play a musical instrument have been found to have a thicker *corpus callosum* (the bridge between the two hemispheres of the brain) than nonmusicians, which means they can go back and forth between left- and right-brained thinking even faster.

> *I liked sitting and really listening to all the noises in the playground. It wasn't until I really paid attention that I heard the birds singing in the trees—something I never noticed before.*
>
> —Janis, age 9

MINDFUL
LISTENING
PRACTICE

THE LISTENING GAME

Gather together several different household items with which to make noise. You could use pencils to tap on a hard surface, paper to crinkle, a spoon to bang against a pot, or coins to rattle.

Place them inside a box so that your children can't see what they are.

Ask your children to close their eyes and focus on the sound you're about to make. Take an item out of the box, make a noise with it, and then hide it again. Ask your children what they think made the sound. Repeat with each item in the box. Ask them the following questions:

> Could you listen better when your eyes were closed?
>
> Were you able to maintain your focus on the sound?
>
> Did anything get in the way?

Now it's their turn to find noisy objects. Enjoy the sharing experience—it's fun. Repeat the practice using different objects and diverse sounds, being as creative and light as you can.

SOUNDS IN THE AIR

Pick a spot outside your house and sit down with your children. Set a timer for two minutes. Ask everyone to close their eyes and really try to notice all the sounds in the air. When the time is up, have them open their eyes. Ask them the following questions:

> Could you hear more than usual when your attention was focused?
>
> Did you notice certain sounds getting louder and then softer?
>
> Was there a beginning or an end to a particular sound?

Point out that those sounds are there all the time; we're just never aware of them. Only when we pay attention can we hear. With older children, you can explore the concept of mindful listening and talk to them about how it can help them in their relationships with friends, teachers, coaches, and family members.

LISTENING TO MUSIC

Choose a song that features several different instruments and play a segment of it. Ask if they can identify the different instruments being played. Is there a drum? A piano? A guitar? What can they hear? Then pick another song. Sometimes music brings up different emotions. Does it make them happy? Does it make them sad? Or do they feel like dancing?

ECHOES

Have your child tell you something as you listen carefully, then repeat what you heard back to her. Do the same thing the other way around: ask her to listen carefully while you say something, and have her repeat back what she heard. Take turns switching back and forth several times, practicing with longer and shorter sentences. Ask her afterward what the experience was like. Was it easy or hard? What helped her remain focused on listening?

Reflections

In the 1980s I took part in a television program called *Kids: Listen to Them*, in which dozens of children aged ten to fifteen spent a day with me and a camera crew. As we talked

about their fears and hopes, many beautiful things were revealed in the few hours that we spent together. One boy
spoke of his parents' divorce and how difficult it was for him.
Others talked of similar experiences and offered advice and
comfort about how to get through school during such times,
creating a shared community that offered solace.

During a brief lull, I asked the children if they believed
that what we think and what we feel are two different
things. It was as if I'd shone a light in the room. All the children suddenly became inspired simply because someone
understood what they were going through. Their openness
and honesty made me wonder why children aren't given the
freedom or the forum to speak so frankly more often. As
parents, we let our schedules become so demanding and our
days so filled that we don't find the time to sit down and ask
our children how they feel or show them that we're ready to
listen. At the end of my time filming for the TV program, the
children gathered around and we enjoyed a group hug. It
was hard to say good-bye. "Couldn't we do this again?" they
pleaded. I wished for all our sakes that we could. But we
all have the memory of that day—a day we danced, cried,
laughed, listened to one another, and became more deeply
connected.

MINDFUL SEEING

We move so fast through life that it often seems to flash by us like
a movie. We ask ourselves where the day went. Or the week.
Good heavens, in some cases we ask, Where did the year go?

It's not surprising that we get distracted when we consider how much information we're expected to take in. Thank goodness our brains have a wonderful filtering system or we'd be completely overwhelmed. An estimated 80 percent of the information that our brains have to absorb is visual. The human eye registers more than thirty-five thousand visual images every hour. Paying attention in the face of such bombardment is a serious practice, if not an art.

> *When I really look at something, I can see all sorts of bits I didn't see before, like the wrinkle on my cat's nose.*
>
> —Megan, age 7

Mindful seeing allows us to calm our brains so that we see things in slow motion, with all their stark colors and contrasts. In all the busyness of our lives, this gives us a chance to really notice details. Jon Kabat-Zinn calls it "coming to our senses." When we mindfully look at something, it not only brings us back to ourselves but also quiets everything down, including our heart rate. Somehow, everything gets simpler.

By stepping away from our normal environment, we can often see things more clearly. Going outside to take a breath and look around at the world can make all the difference to our emotional state. In his book *Last Child in the Woods: Saving Our Children from Nature-Deficit Disorder*, Richard Louv writes, "Nature inspires creativity in a child by demanding visualization and the full use of the senses. Given a chance, a child will bring the confusion of the world to the woods, wash it in the creek, turn it over to see what lives on the unseen side of that confusion."

As parents, mindful seeing also helps us open our hearts. It takes us out of the state of being ever critical and fixes us to a place of peace and appreciation. By choosing to focus on what's true and wonderful about our children, it can help defuse our anger and frustration. We notice instead their vulnerability and tenderness.

We ponder their potential. They grow up fast, and there is so much beauty to observe in them along the way. That's something really worth seeing.

> *The mindful seeing practice helped me at school. Now I really look into all four corners of the computer screen if I don't understand something, and that's helped me find my way around.*
>
> —Maryvel, age 10

Mindful seeing is more important than ever for our children because it neutralizes the frantic nature of their lives. It helps them to slow down and attend to the subtleties. Really looking at something also helps them build attention to visual detail, which is crucial for accuracy in reading, writing, and other schoolwork.

MINDFUL
SEEING
PRACTICE

REALLY LOOKING

Gather together a few pebbles that look much the same and put them in a box or a paper bag. You could also use leaves, buttons, flowers, or anything that has a similar appearance. Ask your child to reach into the box or bag and pick one of the objects. Pick one yourself and do the exercise as well.

Encourage your child to be as quiet and still as possible and then study his object. What does it look like? What colors or markings can he see? Is it smooth or rough? If his mind wanders, tell him that it's okay. Encourage him to bring his attention back to his object and continue noticing everything about it.

Put your objects back in the box or bag. Shake it up. Tip the contents onto the floor and ask your child to try to find the object he was just holding. How easy was it to pick out on the floor? Was it hard to stay focused on it? What did he notice about mindful seeing? Tell him what you noticed, too.

BE AN EXPLORER OF THE WORLD

Take your child out into the yard or to a park. Maybe sit on the front porch. You can also do this indoors if you want. Either way, it's a fun game to play. Once she is quiet and settled, ask her to look around as if she were seeing everything for the first time. Have her pick one object, focus on it for a few minutes, and not say what it is. Close your eyes and have your child describe her object to you. See if you can guess what it is. Take turns picking objects and guessing.

EYE SPY

Try to incorporate mindful seeing into your daily routine. You can play this game on the way to school or the grocery store or perhaps when walking to a friend's house. Get your children to look around them. Ask them to talk about what they see and point out things they never noticed before. Share your own thoughts.

THE SHAPE OF WATER

Another fun exercise is to fill a large clear jar with water. Take some food dye, add a few drops to the water, and watch it disperse into all kinds of shapes and swirls. Talk about what each of you sees in the colored water. Is there the shape of an animal in there? A tree? Maybe a face? Ever since I was small I've played a similar game: lying down and looking at the clouds to see if I can identify creatures emerging from the swirling mists in the sky. Try that with your children, too.

SEEING WITH NEW EYES

Gather some paper and crayons and sit with your child. Ask him to draw something in the room. You pick an object and do this, too. Once he's finished drawing, ask him to study his object in detail. Then ask him to draw the same object again, then to see if there are any differences between his first and second drawings. Did mindful seeing change the drawing in any way?

Reflections

I first learned how to see mindfully after I met the actress Julie Christie while filming *Shampoo* together in the 1970s. When the movie ended, we remained friends. She'd call me from where she lived in England and tell me how beautiful the sky looked or how sparkling the sea was. She'd send me little pen and ink drawings of the view from her Welsh pasture. They were detailed and fine. I could tell that she was deeply focused on what she was seeing. She taught me the importance of paying attention to the small things that we may never otherwise notice, like "the millions of little diamonds that made the ocean so pretty." She refined my eye. Now I live near the ocean, and sometimes when I'm feeling overwhelmed, I go stand at the water's edge and really look at the waves. As I search for those diamonds Julie wrote to me about all those years ago, I breathe deeply and am grateful for the moment, happy to be able not just to look but to really see, and then—of course—to feel.

MINDFUL SMELLING

Remember how the scent of the pine filling the living room on Christmas morning made you feel? How about the smell of wood smoke from the fire welcoming you home on a windy autumn night? Or your father's aftershave? Our sense of smell is the most wonderful thing. It has a direct channel to our memories and emotions.

My mother's perfume was Yardley's lavender, and every night before I go to sleep I put a few drops of lavender oil on my pillow, take a deep breath, and drift to sleep with a deep sense of well-being. We can all remember bad smells, too, usually because they alerted us to harm or danger. Things like gas escaping from the home; food gone bad; sickness on the breath of a child; or oil leaking from an engine. Being able to smell and then remember what any particular scent means and whether it signifies comfort or danger is a vital human skill.

The olfactory gland is not only the strongest gland in the body

> *Smell is rather different from the other senses, as it has a strong, subconscious input to the brain. . . . Smell evokes the emotions surrounding an experience. It can prompt and even re-create those emotions. That is a pretty exclusive function of smell when compared to the other senses.*
>
> —Tim Jacob, professor

but also the greatest trigger of memory and the one that has the biggest impact on our emotional state. Because of this, it helps us with recall and other attributes. One study at Harvard University found that students exposed to the scent of roses as they slept could remember more data than those who weren't. The scent relaxed the brain and stimulated the part responsible for forming long-term memories.

Flower, plant, and herb essences are especially important in this kind of aromatherapy. Lavender and rosemary improve recall. Lemon energizes. Pine calms. Jasmine improves problem-solving abilities. Peppermint can boost everything from memory and concentration to physical performance in athletes. German scientists found that floral scents gave people pleasant dreams, while the smell of rotten eggs gave them bad ones.

At one school in Liverpool, England, teachers release the scent of mint in classrooms during lessons. They combine it with the sounds of leaves rustling and gently trickling water, enlisting the sense of hearing as well. Other educators and scientists have discovered that if they release a particular scent when pupils are learning new information and then rerelease it during the exam on that subject, memory is enhanced. Some innovative schools have introduced "scratch and sniff" cards for just this purpose.

Reflections

My mother had a very good "smeller," as she used to say of her nose. One Thanksgiving, I noticed that she kept opening and closing the oven door. I wondered what was wrong with her. Finally I asked, "Mommy, why do you keep sticking your head in the oven?" She frowned and growled, "I don't think this turkey smells right." She asked me to put my head in the hot oven, too. "Does it smell right to you?" she asked. I honestly didn't know what to say. Then she called my father to come downstairs. He told her it smelled fine, but it didn't end there. One by one the rest of the family was summoned. "No, it's fine," replied one. "Oh, I'm not sure," said another. To my embarrassment, Mom then called in our neighbors for their opinions. Finally one told her, "You know, Laura? This turkey doesn't smell good." My mother nodded, as if she knew that all along. She opened the oven door, picked up our much-anticipated Thanksgiving dinner, and threw it into the trash. As we ate all the trimmings instead, we laughed and laughed about her famous sense of smell. Even without a turkey, that was one of the best Thanksgivings we ever had. I still refer to it as "the Smelling Thanksgiving." Even now, many years later, the scent of a turkey cooking brings back joyful memories. I must have inherited my mother's abilities because of all my senses, smell is the one that lifts and calms my spirit. My father used to say, "Goldie, don't forget to smell the roses." Now I have a rosebush planted right outside my front door in which I bury my "smeller" every time I pass.

MINDFUL
SMELLING
PRACTICE

WHAT'S THAT SMELL?

Choose four things that have distinct and very different smells. Have some fun choosing—maybe pick a pine branch, a stick of cinnamon, a rose, a jar of peanut butter, a sprig of lavender, or some vanilla extract.

Blindfold your children or have them close their eyes, then ask them to take a deep breath and smell each item, one at a time. Ask if they can identify what each is. Do they prefer some smells over others? Do any of the smells make them think of other things? Then have them pick something for you to smell, too.

Continue experimenting like this and ask your children if they find it gets easier to identify smells. Do different smells evoke different memories for them? Share a favorite memory you associate with a particular smell, such as that of a baby, which reminds you of when they were young, or how the scent of freshly baked cookies takes you back to being with your own mother.

If your children can't recall any memories associated with smells, encourage them with suggestions such as, "Remember when we were at the ocean and you picked up that dead fish?" or "What about the time we ran together through the wild sage?"

THE JELLY BEAN TASTE GAME

Gather together some flavored jelly beans. Have your children pinch their noses with their fingers and close their eyes. Give each a jelly bean to taste and ask them to guess the flavor. Then have them unplug their noses and taste the same flavor of jelly bean again. Make sure you take a turn, too. Is it easier to tell the flavor when they can also smell it?

SMELL AND TASTE
At the dinner table, ask your children to smell each bite of food before they put it in their mouths. Does mindful smelling change the way the food tastes?

CAN I EAT THIS?
Collect three food items—like an apple, a bread roll, and a cookie—and three nonfood items—such as laundry detergent, a candle, and hand lotion. Blindfold your children or have them close their eyes, then have them smell each item. Ask them to identify which items they can eat and which they can't. And then have them pick something for you to smell as well.

MINDFUL TASTING

We all enjoy the taste of food. The trouble is that some of us enjoy it too much. The United States is currently in the grip of an obesity epidemic that is especially affecting our children. A staggering 74 percent of adults are overweight or obese, and as many as 25 percent of children. And the figures are rising steadily, according to the Centers for Disease Control and Prevention.

Once we learn to eat mindfully, we will savor every mouthful and tend to eat less. Becoming aware of the importance of chewing our food to aid digestion is another beneficial side effect. Children are fascinated to learn that they should eat a little slower because it takes the brain ten minutes to experience the feeling of being full. Savoring is all the more important because research shows that we have tasted the best of any meal after the second mouthful. That's hard to believe when I'm eating my mother's coconut cake! But perhaps just knowing this can help us walk away from the table not quite so stuffed.

> *Mindful eating involves all the senses. It immerses us in the colors, textures, scents, tastes, and even sounds of drinking and eating. It allows us to be curious and even playful as we investigate our responses to food and our inner cues to hunger and satisfaction.*
>
> —Jan Chozen Bays, MD

The best part about mindful tasting is that it reinforces the pleasures of sitting down and sharing a meal together. This is such an important bonding time and one that I make sure happens regularly in my family. If you don't have that culture, you can still sit with your children while they're eating, engaging them in chat and even doing some mindful exercises while they chew.

Mindful tasting is one of the ways in which we can experience the optimal state of relaxed awareness by paying attention to what we eat. Teaching our children to become fully aware of not only what they're eating but how they're eating helps them recognize what is good and not good for them and take responsibility.

Reflections

I was fourteen years old. My dad was puttering in the kitchen making hush puppies, a throwback from his youth in the

South. He was beating the batter and recalling the best hush puppies he had ever eaten, in a roadside café on one of his cross-country car trips. He then sauntered over and ran his glass under the faucet and filled it up with crystal clear water. He took a long drink, his blue eyes all aflame, and exclaimed, "Go-Go, never stop appreciating a good glass of water!" At fourteen I didn't quite catch his drift. It was just eccentric Daddy. However, these days, long after he has left my world, I get it, and I always remember to keep mindful when I taste tap water in all its glory and appreciate every drop.

MINDFUL
TASTING
PRACTICE

LOOK AND TASTE

Give your children a raisin or a small piece of chocolate. Ask them to hold it and wait. Encourage them to look closely at what's in their hands, as if they've never seen it before. What do they see? What shape is it? What about texture? And color?

Tell them to close their eyes and smell it. What does it remind them of? Was it the last time they ate a raisin or chocolate, maybe? Then ask them to put the morsel

> I was busy so I took my kids to a fast-food restaurant, where they gobbled their food as usual. My younger son started stealing the other's fries. Finally, my older son told him, "You'd better taste that one mindfully because it's the last one you're getting!" I had to laugh!
> —A MindUP mom

in their mouths, just resting on their tongues. Then tell them they can bite down and chew slowly. How does it taste? What does it feel like? Did their mouths water when it was on their tongues? Was it easy or difficult to stay focused and not gobble up the treat?

WHAT DO YOU CALL IT?

Ask your children to choose from a list of taste-related words to describe their experience. You can use the following list or have them add their own words.

- Bitter

- Chewy

- Crunchy

- Fruity

- Salty

- Sweet

- Yucky

- Yummy

Repeat the practice, using different foods each time. Make it a family affair and practice mindful tasting at the dinner table. Pick one item, such as a carrot, and have everyone examine it before they eat it. I know that in my family this would sure elicit some laughs! Then eat it and describe what it tastes like. Is it sweet or sour? Does it taste like it has sugar in it? Another time, have everyone take just one bite from each item on their plate. What were all the different tastes?

IMAGING THE TASTE

Ask your children to imagine that they're holding a lemon and to describe what it looks like. Now get them to imagine that the lemon has been cut into slices. What does it smell like? Ask them to imagine bringing a slice of that lemon to their lips and putting it into their mouths. What happened when they imagined biting into it? Could they taste its sourness? Did their mouths pucker up or their noses wrinkle? Remind them that even though there was no lemon, their mouths still puckered up just thinking about it. What power the imagination has even to create physical responses!

MINDFUL MOVEMENT

Have you ever sat in your office or your living room and felt like you had to get up and move your body or you were going to jump out of your skin? I have. I am a dancer who lives for movement of any kind. It raises my energy, happiness, relaxation, you name it. The act of moving or challenging my body changes my mind state completely.

Our bodies and minds are so closely connected. Movement has many positive effects, including the emission of dopamine—that wonderful neurotransmitter that helps us experience a sense

> Dopamine release (and the pleasure associated with it) has been found highest in children when they are moving, laughing, interacting.
>
> —Judy Willis, MD, MEd

of well-being. Physical activity stimulates all kinds of neural circuits that help our brain and bring loads of benefits, including:

- Improved memory

- Easing of depression

- Improved cognitive ability and problem solving

- Release of neurotransmitters that alleviate both physical and mental pain

- Enhanced neurogenesis, or the creation of new neurons in the brain

So go out for that much-needed run or whatever exercise you like. You will feel better, actually have more energy, and be better able to cope with the day's stresses. This improved sense of well-being helps alert us to the dangers of stress and fatigue. Becoming self-aware is the first step in taking care of ourselves.

Reflections

I've been dancing since I was three. I can honestly say that the highest points in my life, and when I've felt most joyful and integrated with everything around me, have been when I was moving my body to music. The method I learned required that we not only had to perform a pirouette, for instance, but also had to break down the movements to describe how each part of the body was connected to the next. It worked beautifully in integrating the two hemispheres of my brain and connecting my body and mind. On one night in particular, I was performing in *West Side Story* in a theater in Baltimore. Time stood still. I felt I was dancing with the air, with the molecules of the unseen. I felt completely joyful, peaceful, purposeful, and exalted.

Mindful movement can be anything from vigorous or aerobic activity, like riding a bike, running, or hiking in the mountains, to something less taxing, like walking the dog, playing table tennis, or swimming. Doing things together as a family is better still.

MINDFUL
MOVEMENT
PRACTICE

THE PULSE GAME

Sit with your children and show them where to put their two fingers on their wrist in order to find their own pulse. Count the beats together.

Then tell everyone to jump up and down, run around, get excited, scream and shout. Shake your bodies. Do high kicks. Have fun with it. Do this for a minute or two, then sit down on the ground cross-legged and have everyone check their pulse again. See how much faster your hearts are beating. Then have everyone take three long deep breaths in and out.

While they're doing their mindful breathing exercises, have

> *Exercise, novelty, emotional engagement, and optimal states of attention arousal are each ingredients that promote neural plasticity.*
>
> —Daniel J. Siegel, MD

them see how quickly they can bring their pulse down and return to a state of calm. Talk about how long it took them to feel relaxed, share the differences between being calm and being excited, and discuss how we can all manage ourselves when we get overstimulated. Talk to your children about how much we are in control of our bodies.

FREEZE AND MELT

Play a game with your kids called Freeze and Melt. Have them run around wildly then stop whenever you call out "Freeze!" Make

> *Our twins came home and made us turn off the TV and get up off the couch. Then they put on some music and made us dance. I can't remember the last time we had so much fun.*
>
> —A MindUP mom

sure they tense their entire bodies and freeze on the spot. When you call "Melt!" have them relax and slowly melt to the ground. What did they notice when they were freezing? How did it differ from the feeling of melting? Trade places so that you get to do it, too.

PAYING ATTENTION TO EVERY STEP

Whenever you're taking a hike or walking around the park, stop and ask your children to pay attention to their movement for a few minutes. Tell them to really notice their feet lifting up and down and the sensation of moving forward. What did they think was the difference between normal walking and walking mindfully? Were they able to pay more attention?

THE STORK GAME

Find a space where everyone can move around without bumping into anything. Ask your children to stand still and center themselves by breathing. Then ask them to balance on one leg, like a stork. If they lose their balance, laugh with them and ask them to try again. Suggest they focus on a single point or an object. After a few seconds, tell them to stand on both feet, then ask them how their body feels. Switch sides so that they are balancing on their other leg for a few seconds. Was it equally easy to balance on each leg? What were their thoughts—did they feel calm or stressed? Was it helpful to focus on one point?

SO YOU THINK YOU CAN DANCE?

Play some music. Move your bodies as crazily as you like, jumping and bouncing together. Dance alone or with each other. Be free and silly. Ask your children if they feel happy. Do their bodies feel loose or tight? Strong or not strong? Share with them how it makes you feel, too.

Reflections

One day, Kate called to tell me that she and my grandson Ryder were coming over to our house to visit. While I was waiting, I put on the radio and began flipping through channels until I came across some seventies dance music. I started to dance with full abandon. In full performance mode, I was high kicking, turning, and jumping, arms flying and head shaking back and forth in complete rapture. I was completely lost in the moment when I happened to glance up. There were my daughter and four-year-old grandson, noses pressed against the glass of the front door. Oh my God, they were watching me go completely wild and insane. I was sweating, laughing, jumping, yelping all by myself, and they saw all of it. I ran to the door and opened it. Ryder said to me, "Go-Go, what are you doing?" We had a big laugh, and Kate said, "Well, that's your Go-Go, Ryder!" We've always been a dancing family. We've been known to get on chairs and tabletops on vacations to dance wildly and laugh heartily together. There is nothing better for the soul.

PUTTING MINDFUL SENSING INTO PRACTICE

My brother enjoyed mindful sensing in school so much that he talked us all into doing it for an entire weekend at home. The most fun part was mindful eating because we had to really taste our food and share the sensations the food gave us.

—Cathy, age 8

The exciting possibilities of using all of our senses to strengthen our brain muscles, increase our focus, and further our understanding are only just being explored. A growing body of research is linking improved all-around performance to the activation of the human senses.

For example, children learning the word *drum* will take it in much more easily if in addition to seeing a picture of a drum they also hear the sound a drum makes. They would be engaged in mindful listening. By giving them letters with which to spell out the word, they can visualize the shape of the word, which will help them recognize it the next time. This would be an exercise in mindful seeing.

Mindful listening helps us attune to the world around us, whether it's by listening to nature to bring us to a place of peace and tranquillity or by listening closely to what someone is saying. As mentioned earlier, listening intently actually stimulates empathy and creates more awareness, helping us to get along better at home, at school, and in the community. It raises the Emotional Quotient and creates greater equanimity in the home and at school. Developing focused mindful listening helps us absorb and remember information. It also allows us to hear shifts in intonation, which can alert us to someone's underlying mood. Being sensitive to these things can not only create empathy but also defuse a difficult situation. Clearly, what we are talking about here is developing a higher EQ.

In *mindful seeing*, the use of color is proving to be profoundly influential in learning as well. Colors produce electromagnetic radiations, each with its own wavelength. "I'm feeling blue," we sometimes say, and everyone knows that means we're sad. Colors can directly influence how we feel and thus how we take in new information and retain it. Experiments with classrooms painted in various colors found that pupils had higher test scores in rooms painted in earth colors than in those painted in monochrome or black and white. Blue was found to be the most tranquil hue, with green second. Yellow inspired optimism; soft lighting had a similar effect.

Mindful smelling stimulates the memory, and the olfactory gland is the strongest sensory gland in the body. Scent opens up the neural pathways to the limbic system (the emotional brain). Aromas recalled from the past can be a tremendous comfort in times of stress or sadness. Many studies have been done on the effects of scent on our state of mind. And it has been shown that aromatherapy can be used to stimulate the mind and body connection.

Mindful tasting is especially helpful in dealing with those children—and adults—who have eating disorders. According to the AACAP, as many as 10 percent of young women suffer from eating disorders, ranging from obesity to anorexia nervosa or bulimia. Many of them simultaneously suffer from anxiety and depression and have issues with self-esteem. By helping them develop their own senses and teaching them to savor their food, mindfulness training can support greater impulse control and break a cycle of self-abuse.

Mindful movement is important for many things. It helps develop our bodies and keep them in good physical shape. It helps our brains work in symphony because as we move mindfully, many parts of the brain are exercised simultaneously. Developing a strong body creates confidence, allowing us to enter a room fully present, with openness and strength.

All of the aspects of our mindful sensing—listening, seeing, smelling, tasting, and movement—have a direct relationship to neurological development as well as strengthening our ability to focus. By becoming fully aware of all that we can hear, see, smell, taste, and feel, we open up our minds and bodies to the gifts of our senses, which we were born with but may have lost along the way.

Optimism

Optimism is the faith that leads to achievement.
Nothing can be done without hope and confidence.

—Helen Keller

Reflections

From the age of eleven, whenever someone asked me what I wanted to be when I grew up, I'd say simply, "Happy." They looked confused. Maybe I'd misunderstood their question. "Oh, Goldie, that's sweet, honey, but I mean . . . what do you want to be? Don't you want to be a professional dancer?" "No," I said, "I just want to be happy." Upon reflection, even I am amazed that such a lofty wish was a priority for me back then. I guess I was afraid that as I grew up I'd be robbed of the tickle inside me. Did being a grown-up mean that I'd have to abandon my free spirit? I didn't want to grow up to become an adult who never burst into song for no reason or made funny faces in the grocery store. As I grew older, my intention to keep my joy became even stronger; I honestly felt that it was the one thing that was my own and that no one could steal, and when I felt that someone was trying to undermine that gift, I would clearly walk in the other direction. I had found that the most important thing in my life, which had helped create resilience, was the clear intention to be happy.

Imagine two people lost on a mountain trail. One is worried about being lost forever, and the other is just enjoying the view, confident that they'll find their way home. It is a classic example of optimism and pessimism. One hopes for the best and can see the beauty all around them. The other fears the worst and can't see beyond those fears. Another more commonly used example is a half glass of water. Do we see it as *half full* or *half empty*? How we answer that question indicates how happy, healthy, and resilient we are.

> Now whenever I get angry or upset, I take a deep breath and say to myself, "Jar half full, jar half full," until my negative feelings go away.
>
> —George, age 7

One definition of *optimism* is the tendency to interpret events or actions in the best possible light, while *pessimism* is the inclination to interpret the worst. Note the word *interpret*. It is the meaning we place on something that determines whether we feel good or bad about it, not the event itself.

It has been said that we each have a happiness set-point that is established in childhood and remains with us throughout our lives, inflexible to change. This assumption has been clinically proven to be false. Adopting such a stance, however, can be self-fulfilling. For instance, if we repeatedly tell ourselves that things won't work out, they probably won't. Sonja Lyubomirsky, professor of psychology at the University of California, studied sad and happy people, specifically how they perceive themselves and others, and found that if an unhappy person wants to experience joy, then he or she can do so simply by learning the habits of happy people.

Furthermore, Dr. Lyubomirsky discovered that happiness has numerous positive by-products that benefit not only the individual but society at large. These include:

> *The plasticity of connections between the thinking and feeling regions of the brain casts doubt on the belief that each of us has a "setpoint" for happiness, and that neither a sports win nor a national tragedy budges it for long. If inhibitory connections between the frontal lobes and the amygdala can be strengthened in an enduring way, then perhaps you can voluntarily shift that not-so-set-point.*
> —Sharon Begley

- A longer and more satisfying marriage

- A larger number of friends

- Increased energy

- The ability to earn a higher income

- The chance for a better career

- Richer social interactions

- Better physical health

Positive psychologist Dr. Barbara L. Fredrickson asked herself a simple question: If we know that negative emotions help focus our attention and spur us into action to protect us from dangerous situations, then what purpose do positive feelings serve? After years of research at the University of North Carolina, she determined that *positive emotions undo the effects of the negative ones*, quelling physical reactivity. Like a reset button, they allow our bodies and minds to come back into emotional and physical balance. Position One.

Fredrickson's research (along with hundreds of similar studies) shows that experiencing positive emotions not only reflects contentment with our lives but predicts success in relationships and careers. She calls her theory of positive emotions "broaden-and-build" because feeling optimism, gratitude, and joy *broadens* our minds, helping us *build* a more productive future.

We already know that negative, angry, or pessimistic thoughts activate the amygdala in the brain, turning on the stress response to flood our body with the hormones that depress our mood. When we think positive thoughts, such as gratitude, kindness, and optimism, we get a surge of the neurotransmitter dopamine, helping us with attention, motivation, and perseverance. I call them "dopamine bubbles."

What's more, through the release of another hormone, called DHEA, and proteins that regulate the immune response, our immune systems are strengthened, something that has been linked to alleviating the symptoms of anything from psoriasis to back pain, diabetes, fibromyalgia, and arthritis.

These feel-good chemicals even help with the common cold. The more positive we are, the less likely we are to become ill. Positive emotions also increase pain tolerance through the release of the brain's own morphinelike substances.

So, without being aware of it, and purely by positive thought, we and our children can inject our bodies and minds with these mood-enhancing and health-altering chemicals. Research by Richard Davidson, PhD, professor of psychology and psychiatry at the University of Michigan, has found that these chemicals actively promote cell growth, while those released by negative emotions speed cell decay. Similar studies have found that pessimists are three times more likely to develop high blood pressure and heart disease than are optimists. And depression can almost double our risk of dementia later in life, according to a study published in the journal *Neurology*.

Optimists even live longer. One study of patients at the Mayo Clinic found that those of us who remain happy live 19 percent longer than those who are pessimists. Other studies have confirmed this. This is why it is so vital to nurture these skills in our children. Just imagine what effect there might be on the health care system of the future if our children learn to implement these tools to foster such positive benefits at a young age.

Reflections

One day when I was being driven to work in the middle of a particularly stressful time for me, I caught sight of myself in the rearview mirror and noticed that my eyes were dead; there was no life in them, no joy. That was just not acceptable. I did this little exercise: I decided to pretend I had just landed from Mars and was looking at the trees and the houses for the very first time. I focused on the nature all around me and conjured feelings of wonder and awe. Mind you, I'm not crazy; this was just an exercise. I looked mindfully at the trees and saw shapes and colors I'd noticed before, even though I had taken that same route for thirty years. Something extraordinary happened. I noticed the corners of my mouth turning up. I was smiling; I was present. I suppose one could describe this as a transformational experience. My driver pulled up next to my dressing room trailer at work, and I jumped out of the car, completely energized. I plopped myself into the makeup chair, and my makeup artist said, "Well, you're in a good mood today. What happened to you?" I laughed and said I just looked at the trees for the first time.

Optimism acts like a resiliency vaccine that enables us to bounce back from emotional and physical difficulties more easily. It used to be believed that some people were just naturally more resilient than others. Recent research, however, shows that we all have the capacity to rebound from challenges. It's a matter of holding positive attitudes, which include seeing a negative situation as an opportunity for growth, focusing on a brighter future, practicing gratitude, and laughing as much as possible whenever possible.

All this may sound too good to be true, but it is backed up with more and more scientific research. Know that we can help ourselves and our children by just thinking positively and behaving with more optimism in every aspect of our lives. Quite apart from the stresses of raising a family, we also have to contend with work, illness, divorce, and financial concerns. Fortunately, there are many simple things we can do to bring ourselves back to a better state of mind and take life day by day in as good a mood as possible. This will guarantee a better future for ourselves and our children.

Positive emotions have the added bonus of allowing us to take in more information and therefore see a wider range of solutions to problems. That's because when we're experiencing stress, our perception narrows to focus solely on the problem.

Without such stress, our perception is widened. Seeing a problem from 100,000 feet up helps us become more aware of different interpretations, more creative in problem solving, and better able to access information.

Here are some other benefits of optimism:

- Doctors in a positive mood are better at diagnosing patients.

- Optimistic office managers are more careful, have greater accuracy in decision making, and are more effective with their teams.

- Students in a good mood before standardized tests do better than those in a bad mood.

In addition, stress and anxiety decrease the ability to retain information in long-term memory for end-of-year exams even if students have achieved good grades in interim tests along the way.

Once children learn to change and control their emotional states, they can manage and reduce their own stress levels. When stress is managed and we learn to live in the present moment, we can become much more productive, more motivated to learn, and better at recall.

Sadly, positive emotions aren't the only things that increase dopamine levels in young people. High-risk behaviors like drinking alcohol, taking drugs, binge eating, driving too fast, and engaging in sex do as well. Teaching children to raise dopamine levels in healthy ways will make them less vulnerable to engaging in dangerous activities.

Playing, laughing, exercising, being optimistic, being kind, showing gratitude, and feeling proud of their achievements are some of the best ways to activate dopamine and the other feel-good opiates and neurotransmitters. No man-made stimulus can trigger them in the same way.

We need to use this knowledge to help our children broaden their thinking and increase the possibility of reaching their true potential.

Reflections

My parents nurtured my optimistic nature, and that helped me cope with life's setbacks. Mildly dyslexic, with a reading comprehension problem, I was placed in the lowest reading group in my class, known as the Purple Balls. I thought that meant I was special. Even when I found out that being in the Purple Balls meant I was supposed to be "dumb," I was never made to feel so. I was a C student whose parents cried "Hallelujah!" if I brought home a B because they knew I'd done my best. They relished my innate happiness and daydreamy nature, never once chastising me for writing "Love Goldie, x" at the end of each (unfinished) paper, or for coloring everything in yellow because that was my favorite color. My parents encouraged my other talents of singing and dancing so that I never felt I was less than they wanted me to be. They saw me for who I really was—the whole me—and then they allowed me the space to realize my truest, happiest self.

Optimism has emotional benefits far beyond giving us more happiness in the moment and more hope for a positive future; it also helps relationships survive.

For a long-lasting, loving relationship, there should be at least one optimist in a pairing, for if two pessimists are together, they are likely to bring each other down. Professors Frank Fincham and Thomas Bradbury, researchers in the field of personal relationships, cognition, and emotion, found that the presence of one optimist prevents a downward spiral of gloom when something difficult occurs. This finding gives us the clue that when our children are feeling pessimistic, we need to inject some optimism into the situation to help create a balanced perspective. (Don't forget to check in on your own emotional state, as you may be unconscious of your own pessimism.)

Researcher Barbara Fredrickson discovered that when we feel good we flourish: We move into an upward spiral of happiness. We become more connected to the people around us and more engaged and satisfied with our lives. In one study, a random group of people were asked to practice a form of attentive mindfulness for eighty to ninety minutes a week (or approximately twelve minutes per day) for nine weeks. Their emotional state was then compared to that of a control group who did nothing. There were few results in the first two weeks, but by the third week, those doing the mindful practice began to feel a rise in positive feelings. By the end of the nine weeks, they were found to be three times happier than they had been before the practice.

"Think of this as getting better and better at squeezing the juice out of an orange," Fredrickson says. "Over time, the people in our study got better and better at extracting the 'joy juice' (through mindful attentiveness)." This finding has been endorsed by teachers using the MindUP program; results may not happen instantly, but over time an atmosphere of positive energy develops. So as we try these practices, we must remember to believe in the positive effects and keep on doing them with our children. Because of plasticity, we will transform our brains toward the positive.

Another important finding Barbara Fredrickson uncovered in her research was that if we increase our practice of positive emotions so that we experience three times as many positive feelings as negative, we pass a tipping point where we begin to truly flourish. This ratio of three to one has been shown to be true for individuals overcoming depression, for happy relationships, and even for high-performing work teams.

> When I had to think about all the people I knew who were pessimists or optimists, I realized that the ones I liked to be with the best were the optimists. If I stay positive, my friends might like me more.
>
> —Cheryl, age 14

Three positives to one negative seems to be the magic number. Below that amount, negativity tends to swamp good feelings; but at three to one or greater, positive emotions are happening enough to generate a sense of general well-being and greater success.

Remember, this is only a ratio. We can't get rid of negative emotion, nor would we want to, because it is an important part of our emotional landscape that shouldn't be suppressed. We all have things to be angry about, sad about, or afraid of. We all have moments where we can't see a happy outcome. Don't ignore them. It's important to spend this time reflecting on the facts and accept when something truly isn't working. Only when we have felt such sorrow can we fully appreciate our joys. Furthermore, it is vital that we feel our more painful emotions, such as mourning the passing of loved ones. It is important to move through our uncomfortable emotions instead of recoiling from them, but we must avoid wallowing in them too long, because that can lead to a more serious state of depression. Creating more positive than negative thoughts fosters greater optimism, which allows us to see a light at the end of our particular tunnel.

MINDFUL
OPTIMISM
PRACTICE

HALF FULL OR HALF EMPTY

Fill a glass jar to the halfway point with jelly beans, cookies, or other favorite treats. Gather your children together, show them the jar, and ask, "Do you think this jar is half empty or half full?"

Talk about the difference of opinion of someone who feels happy looking at the jar compared to someone who feels sad. Suggest different ways those two individuals might respond. The happy, optimistic person might say, "There's still half a jar of jelly beans," while the sad, pessimistic person might look at the same jar and take a negative view by saying, "Oh no, the jelly beans are almost all gone."

TAKING A POSITIVE PERSPECTIVE

If your child is playing soccer or a similar game but hasn't scored a goal in some time, ask her what she thinks would be a negative way to look at the situation. Maybe she'd say things like, "I'm no good at soccer. I don't want to play anymore." Now talk about the situation from a positive perspective. Ask what she likes most about playing the game. Is it being part of a team, or maybe running around outside? Does she like seeing her friends the most? Or is it the possibility of scoring a goal in the future? Finally, ask her which she believes is the better way of thinking. Which would she like to be in the future—an optimist or a pessimist?

These kinds of questions can be used in almost everything you do with your children—such as reading a book or watching TV together. Which character or person appears to be optimistic? Who is pessimistic? You can also apply it to something your children are experiencing currently, like struggling to keep up with their homework or having a difficult time with a sibling. Encourage them to look at the positive in the situation. Remind them how good it feels when they've finished their homework and received a high grade. Ask them to list what they most like about their sibling.

Make a list of people you know from among your friends, family, and neighbors. Ask your children which ones they think are optimists and which are pessimists. How can they tell?

RAINY DAY BLUES

Pretend that it's raining outside. Take turns feeling sad or happy about the rain. Act out a positive response together, such as jumping up and down in puddles or throwing back your head to feel the rain on your face. How did each charade make them feel? Have fun with them. They'll get this.

SING A HAPPY SONG

Whenever the radio is on, ask your children if the song that is playing is a happy or a sad song. Does it make them feel like dancing or sitting quietly? If it is a sad song, ask them how it makes them feel. When there's a happy song on, dance with your children. Keep it light and fun. Which songs make them most happy? Always end the practice playing a happy song to finish on an upbeat note.

10

Happiness

*We need to remind ourselves that many pleasurable moments
exist each day in our life. Understanding this, we make a
decision to start noticing them. We take a few seconds here, a
moment there, to stop and appreciate the small joys and
beauty in our lives. And far from it being a chore, we find
ourselves refreshed by this simple practice.*

—John Kehoe, *The Practice of Happiness*

Writing about happiness makes me happy, and focusing on happiness is not a frivolous pursuit; it is one of the emotions that can inform the trajectory of our lives. Life can be hard, and some believe it can get harder as time goes on. One of the times in our lives when our happiness can be greatly challenged is when we are raising our children. I can remember always feeling tired and wondering if I would ever return to the sexy, vibrant person I was before having children. It is a nonstop proposition, being a parent, but I found that the stresses of raising a family can only steal your happiness if you allow them to. Be on guard with your emotional state:

- Don't get hijacked by anger.

- Remain in the present and be aware.

- Try to be optimistic and see the good side.

- Practice gratitude.

- Forgive.

Use whatever mindful tools you can to lift your spirits, put a smile back on your face, and change your brain. We've all heard the expression "Count your blessings," and it really works. All you have to do is try to catch yourself whenever you think a negative thought and look for evidence in your life to the contrary. This way you create optimism not just for the sake of it but to be grounded in reality.

We can help our children think similarly, not only by being role models of positivity for them but also by helping them to savor happiness themselves. Remember, the more a thought is practiced, the stronger the circuits that hold it in memory become. When we and our children repeatedly imagine happy outcomes instead of negative ones, our brains build resilience, perseverance, and insurance against depression. It is what psychologists call creating *intention*, *attention*, and *attitude*.

Depressed teenagers taught to practice mindful optimism three times a day were able to significantly reduce anxiety and depression and improve self-esteem and sleep quality. This was reported by Shauna Shapiro in a study of mindfulness-based stress reduction in northern California.

When we savor happiness, it's pretty much what it sounds like. Just as in mindful tasting, we never want that juicy peach to end. We hold it, we value it, we spend time with it in unhurried appreciation. This prolongs the enjoyment of it. Positive psychologists are fascinated by what raises our mood, but it was Aristotle who identified two pathways to conscious happiness:

■ **Fulfillment:** Using our gifts and talents on behalf of what matters to us

■ **Contentment:** Experiencing pleasurable moments and being satisfied with life

Savoring happy experiences falls into the contentment category. We often think that acquiring new toys, gadgets, or whatever will make us happier. This phenomenon is known as the hedonistic treadmill. A new toy, even a new car, is exciting for a while as the dopamine kicks in, but eventually the brain gets familiar with the new toy and searches for something new. The little bites of feel-good just don't last. Children today are often caught up in this cycle of "Got to have it! Got it! Want something else!" At times we feel frustrated by their need for the new and different, but we need to look at our own lives and see where they have learned this behavior. It sometimes feels like nothing is ever enough.

This "never enough" syndrome is counteracted by savoring. It encourages our brains to pay attention to what we have and give it lasting effect and meaning. This is because our dopamine output increases not only when we experience something pleasurable the first time but again when we remember it—so we get a double dose. Best of all, we and our children can enjoy more of what we already have.

Reflections

One of the most joyful times Kurt and I had was the first time we saw Kate and Oliver onstage together. They were in their annual school production, *Alice in Wonderland*. Kate, who was eight, was given the part of Alice. Oliver, who was eleven, was playing Tweedledum. Kurt and I sat in the audience, nervously holding each other's hands, anticipating the entrance of little Kate. She emerged in all her glory; a bigger performance we had never seen. Clearly she had found her spot in life, no surprise to us. She glided, arms outstretched, from one corner of the stage to the other. Her joy at being in the limelight was apparent. I looked at Kurt, and we were doubled over with joy. She was as cute as a button and larger than life, just the beginning of what was to come. Then, alas, Mr. Oliver graced the stage. He looked hilarious in his homemade costume, sporting an umbrella. We witnessed his natural comedic timing and gifts as soon as he tried to open his umbrella: it jammed and would not open on cue. Kurt and I stopped breathing. He tried again and failed. Oliver took a moment, gave a look to the audience—a crooked smile—did a little whoop-de-do with his prop, and brought the entire house to its knees. He was completely fearless. That was one of those seminal moments of shared joy and happiness that made us savor all that we had and appreciate every moment. Even writing about it now brings up all the joy bubbles again. Memories can do that. My double dose.

Savoring, as defined by Fred Bryant and Joseph Veroff of Loyola University, gives us the capacity to attend to our joys, pleasures, and other positive feelings. Savoring is vital to love, friendship, physical and mental health, creativity, and spirituality. Put simply, it expands our heart's capacity for joy.

Bryant and Veroff discovered that there are five ways to best experience the savoring of happiness:

■ **Sharpening perception:** allowing ourselves to really taste food or smell a flower so that we get its full pleasure

■ **Absorption:** immersing ourselves in the experience without thinking about what else we should be doing, how the situation could be better, or what will happen next

■ **Self-congratulation:** taking pride in something that goes well; acknowledging how hard we worked or how long we've waited; having no shame in celebrating success when we've earned it

■ **Sharing with others:** retelling a happy event so that our brains relive the experience and release the feel-good chemicals again

■ **Memory building:** taking photographs or collecting souvenirs of happy events—each time we look at them, we experience the happiness we first knew

MINDFUL
HAPPINESS
PRACTICE

It's good to make the intention to find some time in your frenzied day to sit quietly with your children and talk. Talk about the fun times you've shared, such as walking on the beach, taking a family vacation, or celebrating a birthday. You will be amazed at what you will collectively recall of the wonderful moments and at how you can relive them again by just "sitting and talking on the stoop," as I like to call it. Just talking about the events actually brings back those feelings of happiness as if they were happening at that very moment.

> *Abundant moments often go unnoticed and unappreciated. We need to make an effort to see them and capture them in awareness, and we have to continually work at it because the mind is so easily veiled from fullness at any moment by so many other things.*
>
> —Jon Kabat-Zinn, PhD

THE HAPPY WALL

Sit down with your children and get some crayons or colored pencils and draw pictures of their happy memories. Create a Happy Wall on which to hang the pictures. Choose somewhere that you walk by every day.

Gather together some magazines, scissors, paper, and glue. Create a collage illustrating some of your happiest family experiences, or just paste together random pictures of people having fun together. Add these to your Happy Wall. It's all yours; be creative and have fun with it.

THINGS TO BE HAPPY ABOUT

Compile a list of the things that make you and your children happy. Start each sentence with "I am happy when I ..." It can be something as simple as eating peanut butter sandwiches or playing in the sprinkler, snuggling up for a bedtime story, or watching a puppy at the pet store. Put your list up on your Happy Wall.

SHARING HAPPY STORIES

Take turns telling stories of something you've done that you feel proud of. Maybe it was a task completed, a test passed, or a cake baked. Ask your children when they felt most proud. Celebrate that success again and share in the glory of the moment.

MAKING A HAPPINESS BOX

Get an empty box and wander around your home and backyard with your children. Gather together some small items that make each of you feel good or that capture happy memories. They might be shells or photographs, stickers or heart-shaped rocks. Put the things in the Happiness Box and put it in a special place. Remind them that when they need cheering up, they can always open their box and be reminded of happier moments.

SAVORING HAPPINESS
DAY BY DAY

Perhaps the most important thing optimism and savoring happiness can do is prevent depression, because they exercise areas of our brains that make us less likely to get depressed, even when facing hard times.

When the brains of optimistic people are scanned by an fMRI, they are seen to light up differently when they think about the future than those of pessimists. One of the areas that lights up is precisely the same area that is underactive when someone is depressed, according to psychologist and neuroimaging specialist Tali Sharot.

After my mom died, my dad and I created an album of photos of her always smiling. Whenever one of us is sad, we sit and look through the album together and talk about all the happy times we spent with her. I love that book.

—Kyle, age 9

Not only is there a strong link between pessimism and depression, but pessimists are up to eight times more likely to become depressed. In a thirty-year study, Dr. Martin Seligman of the University of Pennsylvania researched why depression has become such an epidemic in the last few decades. He proved that teaching ten-year-old children the skills of optimistic thinking cut in half their chances of becoming depressed while going through puberty. These years are some of the most difficult for our children, and they need balance and perspective as their hormones and untamed amygdala conspire against them.

Whenever children feel pessimistic, especially in their teens, they regard any negative comments made by others as evidence of their worthlessness rather than just someone else's opinion.

Optimism prevents such teasing from becoming devastating. Pessimistic children also tend to avoid effort because they constantly expect failure. How many times have we heard our children literally talking themselves into failure by saying things like, "I can't do this!" or "It's too hard!" or "I'll never be able to finish this!" It's easy to feel helpless in the face of such comments. Fortunately, optimism can influence our children's belief in themselves for the better as well as their willingness to approach challenges.

The best news is that optimism can be learned. Dr. Seligman also discovered that change starts with understanding how we explain good and bad events. When something bad happens, pessimists tell themselves the three Ps:

- They introduce the *personal* by saying, "It's all my fault."

- They bring on the *permanent* by thinking, "It's always like this."

- They add the *pervasive* with thoughts like, "Everything is terrible."

Optimists tell themselves the opposite: They start with the impersonal, thinking, "Things I have no control over are to blame." They consider the impermanent—"I'm going through a hard time, but I know it will get better. Sometimes things are hard." Finally, they settle on the specific—"This particular thing is hard for me, but the rest of my life is still good."

Consider, for a minute, whether you are a natural optimist or pessimist. Which are the stories you tell yourself when bad things happen? The answer to that question has tremendous relevance to us as parents. Because, as Dr. Seligman writes in *The Optimistic*

Child, our child is paying attention—particularly when we respond emotionally to a situation.

"When you are upset," he says, "you find yourself explaining the disturbing event to whomever is around: the car got dented because that inconsiderate wretch cut you off; Daddy slammed the door because he's in a bad mood; you can't get a job because the economy stinks; Granny is sick because she's so old. Your explanatory style is on display and your child is listening intently . . . and she is making your style her own."

Of course, other factors—such as teachers, coaches, and single traumatic events—can also influence our child's mood, but to a great extent we hold the responsibility of being the role model they are learning from. This is exemplary of the very theme of this book and why it is necessary to become self-aware, as it is the first step to becoming a mindful parent.

Gratitude

*We can only be said to be alive in those moments when
our hearts are conscious of our treasures.*
—Thornton Wilder

Thank you. Those two little words convey so much. *Thank you* means that you've taken the time out to let someone know that you're grateful for something they've said or done. *Thank you* shows that you are thinking of someone other than yourself. *Thank you* means you care.

Psychologists have discovered that the experience of being thankful or appreciative of someone or something is one of the best ways to increase happiness. An incredible 90 percent of people surveyed found that expressing gratitude made them more joyful; 84 percent said it reduced stress and depression and helped create optimism; and 78 percent said it gave them more energy.

Thankfulness is also one of the keys to being able to bounce back from difficulties and experience less stress in the face of ongoing problems. When we focus on how grateful we are for what's right in our lives, even in the midst of challenges, we recognize that a situation isn't totally bleak and give ourselves the energy to move forward. The more we integrate gratitude, the more we are able to forgive, rather than getting stuck in bitterness and resentment.

The bottom line is that focusing on what's wrong makes us unhappy and unhealthy, while focusing on what's right boosts body, mind, and spirit. Best of all, gratitude is completely free and takes virtually no time to express.

Reflections

I was nineteen years old and had been hired to dance at a dinner club in Puerto Rico. I was excited to be away from home for the first time doing what I loved, but the experience wasn't quite as joyful as I'd imagined it would be. The other dancers and I found out that the singers in the show were being paid much more than we were, and yet we were the ones working longer and harder. I was picked to air our grievances. I pulled myself together and approached our boss nervously. When I told her that the pay scale was unfair and that we wanted a raise, she became so angry that her face turned red, the veins in her neck swelled, and she spewed abusive words at me. She told me I was ugly and stupid with stick-out ears and that I would never get another job. I was so hurt I had to hold back my tears. I walked away to gather my spirit and my thoughts. I just wanted to feel happier. I sat alone and tried to think of the best way to handle my emotions as well as the situation. I told myself how lucky I was that she had even hired me in the first place. I looked at the aquamarine sea and the beach I had frolicked on day after day and how I felt I was in paradise while it was snowing in New York City. I took a deep breath, calmed down, and told myself surely I wasn't the first person she had yelled at, and I wouldn't be the last. My sadness was intercepted by reason and perspective and, of course, the wish to feel better. I no longer carried her anger around with me. I let it go. There is nothing like a burning ambition to be happy to help transform negative emotions into positive ones.

When I first began to read some of the extensive neurological and psychological research on the effects of gratitude, it seemed almost too good to be true. I am now convinced that gratitude is a powerful force for our bodies, minds, and emotions—I call it vitamin G.

Researchers have found that when we are thankful, we love our lives and want to make sure we stick around long enough to enjoy them. People who kept a weekly gratitude journal were found to have fewer physical problems and to feel less pain. They exercised more regularly, ate better, and went for regular checkups. They even put on sunscreen more often than others. In all, thankfulness adds an average of seven years to our lives.

Gratitude works on us emotionally, too. It makes us kinder and more generous to others, better able to cope with stress, and less lonely. Higher levels of gratitude have even been shown to reduce incidences of the following disorders:

- Depression
- Bulimia

- Phobias

- Alcohol and drug dependency

This is powerful information for parents because these are the very traps we fear our children could fall into as teens and young adults. Gratitude has been shown to be very effective in reducing the stress of parenting, particularly in new moms and dads. Talking of new parents, people who practice gratitude report that they have less trouble falling asleep, sleep longer than others, and feel more refreshed in the morning.

Gratitude is also one of the keys to happy relationships. Through research that spanned two decades, marriage and parenting expert Dr. John Gottman discovered that couples who maintain at least the all-important three-to-one ratio of positive to negative feelings were more likely to have long-lasting relationships. Furthermore, he found that it is gratitude that prevents us from taking the other person for granted and focusing only on what's not working between us. Whenever we share our appreciation with someone, not only do we boost our own mood but the people around us feel better, too.

> One of my pupils was suffering from depression. He'd never had a friend due to some language processing problems. During the gratitude practice, he heard how important he was to other boys in the class. The difference was extraordinary, and his parents say he is so much happier and now has children come over to play.
> —Barbara K., a MindUP teacher

If we can focus on gratitude, then, both our attitude and our children's attitude will improve, and this will create a happier household because gratitude permeates everything. Take note of the complaining you do about your child's behavior. Sometimes we can get on a loop with that, and it becomes constant and habituated. If you catch your child doing something right, be conscious of it, praise him, and thank him, because research shows something wonderful—he'll likely try to please you again.

This is because when someone receives praise, the brain releases dopamine, and that encourages the person to try for a second "hit." Remember that there are many different ways of being effective in giving appreciation. General remarks, like "You're great," don't teach the child's brain anything about what he did to win our praise. Sometimes it can undermine his belief in himself. Why not explain how he's great and what positive effect his action had? Say something like, "When you cleared the table without my asking, it helped me stay on schedule and reminded me how considerate you are. Thank you." This kind of encouragement, respect, and praise reinforces what qualities he brought to the situation and how valuable he was.

Grateful individuals place less importance on material goods; they are less likely to judge their own and others' success in terms of possessions accumulated; they are less envious of others; and [they] are more likely to share their possessions with others relative to less grateful persons.

—Robert Emmons and Michael McCullough

Most children aren't naturally thankful, so we have to teach them to cultivate it. We also have to be patient. According to personality psychologist Robert Emmons, children under the age of seven find it hard to understand the concept of gratitude. There are gender differences, too. One study of school-age students after 9/11 found that girls were more likely to be grateful than boys and tended to name family and friends they were thankful for. Boys, on the other hand, were more grateful for material objects.

When encouraging our children to show gratitude, we need to be careful not to judge their choices. It's not *what* they're thankful for but *that* they're thankful that's important.

One of the other great benefits of gratitude is that it helps ignite children's interest in school and family, improves their alertness, and enables them to experience greater satisfaction with their lives generally. Those who are grateful tend to make more progress toward achieving important personal goals.

In one study, students were assigned to one of three groups. Those in the first group were asked to record up to five blessings every day for two weeks; those in the second were instructed to record up to five hassles every day for the same period. The third was a control group and did nothing. The children in the "blessings" group were found to be happier and healthier than those in the control and "hassles" groups after just two weeks, plus they were significantly more optimistic about the upcoming school week and satisfied about school and their lives in general even three weeks later. Now that's a powerful incentive.

> When I asked my class to share what they were thankful for, their responses were amazing. I expected toys, video games, etc., but what I got were things like, I am grateful for my sister and my family; for my mom's hugs; for turkey; for sleeping; for the four seasons. I had tears. The answers were so calm and genuine.
>
> —Mark B., a MindUP teacher

MINDFUL
GRATITUDE
PRACTICE

GRATITUDE JOURNAL

Start a new game called the Gratitude Journal. Every day, when you have time, write down five or more things you're thankful for. You can illustrate it, too.

> *Gratitude diaries can really work. In studies we found that if you manage to write down three things each day that are going well and do it for longer than a week . . . levels of well-being rise even up to six months afterwards.*
>
> —Ilona Boniwell, PhD

You begin with something like, "I'm grateful that I have enough to eat," then draw a picture of some food. Ask your children to write down what they're grateful for. If they get stuck, help them by suggesting their best friend or the family dog. Or maybe something more general, like the sunset or a rainbow, the clouds, or the moon.

When they are drawing or writing about what they're thankful for, encourage them to talk about what makes them so grateful for it. How does it make them feel?

A SYMBOL OF GRATITUDE

Give each of your children a small stone or pebble. Keep one for yourself. Tell them it is their Gratitude Stone. Ask them to carry it in their pocket or schoolbag, and say that every time they feel it with their fingers, they should think of something to be grateful for. Remind them that no matter where they are or what is happening in their lives, if they just touch their stone they'll feel grateful. Try it yourself, too.

GIVING THANKS

Gratitude has many practical applications, not least in dealing with anger, as I did when I was faced with my boss in Puerto Rico. Drawing on my gratitude, I was able to savor the positive parts of my working experience and prevent her from making me feel bad about myself, even if my ears do still stick out!

> *Mindfully counting your blessings is like watering seeds in your heart.*
> —Jon Kabat-Zinn, PhD

Similarly, thankfulness helps us in tough times. We've all made lists of how friends or partners annoy us, using them as a weapon against bad behavior. When we practice gratitude, we can sit down and write a list of what we're grateful for about that person, too, and suddenly things don't seem so bad. Gratitude is the elixir to bring us back to a kinder, gentler state of mind.

Expressing gratitude can be used in so many difficult situations, where our emotions take over and our actions are ruled by our hearts instead of our heads. Stopping to count our blessings isn't just a cliché; it is actually a blessing in itself.

Anger

*For every minute you remain angry you give
up sixty seconds of peace of mind.*

—Ralph Waldo Emerson

We all experience anger, fear, and sadness in our lives. Everyone suffers hardship of some kind or other. It is perfectly normal to experience painful feelings, angry feelings, feelings of resentment. The key, of course, is how we handle those emotions. Negative emotions like these can be extremely destructive, as they blur our vision, disable us, and take us down paths we will surely regret. It is important that we try not to get stuck in negative habits or ruts that can lead to deeper problems in the long run, such as depression or anxiety. It's healthier to try to work out our anger and not overreact to it, so that we can neutralize those emotions in order to think more clearly and create more positive outcomes.

Children have just as difficult a time with these destabilizing emotions and need to be given the skills to deal with them. And we must learn to recognize them in our children because their feelings are sometimes very different from ours. Once again, to be tuned in to our children's emotions is tremendously important. For children especially, there is a chasm between feelings and behavior. It's important for us to understand the difference because children don't necessarily express their emotions directly. Sometimes they don't have the words. Their sadness, fear, or anger is usually only a symptom of something else that is bothering them.

The tantrum of a five-year-old whose parents are going through a divorce may well be sparked by the sense of loss and abandonment that he's feeling. It is an acting-out behavior triggered by his emotions. We have to try not to overreact to the symptoms. Try to help him understand that it's all right to feel anger but it's not all right to express it violently or with cruel words. Once a child's feelings are recognized and dealt with, then the emotional charge can be defused and we can create better and calmer ways to solve problems.

Nip anger in the bud. It is toxic to your relationships, your body, and your health. It shows on your face and can impair your ability to have a happy life. Angry outbursts can become habitual; the more you allow anger to take control, the deeper the brain pathways are carved. I call them the Grand Canyon of Anger. *Anger begets anger*. If your child is hyper and showing signs of frustration and aggression, the worst thing you can do is tell him to go to his room and beat on a pillow or punching bag to get his anger out. That only reinforces the behavior.

> *What you begin to notice as you strengthen [the brain] is the absence of the negative state.*
> —Daniel Goleman, PhD

We've all seen mild outbursts turn quickly into full-blown tirades. As stress hormones like cortisol and adrenaline are released, they only intensify the amygdala's sense of danger, making it increasingly difficult to access the calming executive functions of the prefrontal cortex.

Scientists have found that these inflammatory neurotransmitters of the stress response are released in not one but two stages. The first surge lasts for a few minutes and prepares the body for the usual fight, flight, or freeze response. The second stage lasts longer—from hours to days, depending on how worked up we get. This puts us into a state of overdrive in which we tend to overreact and lash out at everything and anything.

> Being mindful calms me down when I am angry. It helps me not get in a big fight because I don't want to hurt my friends. It also helps me focus on my work.
>
> —Brent, age 11

Both as parents and for our own peace of mind, we need to catch that anger during the first hormonal surge so that we can calm down in time to prevent the second, more destructive surge from occurring. When we pay attention and remember what is happening within our brains, we can break the chain of anger for everyone's well-being.

Reflections

When one of my sons was five years old, I picked him up from nursery school and asked, "How was your day?" He got in the car with his lunchbox and told me, "Robert was very angry today." He wasn't upset, and the fact that his friend was angry didn't seem to bother him. He was merely expressing his viewpoint. I suspected that Robert, a hyperactive child, had probably thrown a tantrum. My five-year-old was able to witness that tantrum and see behind the behavior to the feelings that sparked it. Smiling, I said, "Well, we all get angry sometimes, don't we?" He nodded. I was amazed that instead of being offended, he had a clear perspective that his friend was feeling angry and frustrated for reasons that we may never know. We drove on in silence. I was a proud mother.

One of the most powerful things that children in the MindUP program learn is that emotions come and go. That's the way our brains work. Whatever we are feeling, it's not going to last forever. However, when we're caught up in the storm of a strong emotion, it is hard to remember that it's only temporary.

For example, once we become upset that our child refuses to do his homework, our emotional system fires up and we often can't get out of our own way. Our brains become hell-bent on believing that this lack of application indicates that our child is going to be lazy for the rest of his life. Even if it's only because he stayed out too late the night before, we get ourselves so worked up we can no longer see the whole picture. It's like a skip in an old-fashioned long-playing record—the same line just plays over and over. The fear this produces drives deeper and deeper grooves into the negative thinking in our brains. Wouldn't it be nice if we could change the record?

Mindful practices like breathing and sensing actually reduce the amount of time it takes to calm down. We can think rationally again and see the bigger picture. We can observe how our thoughts and feelings come and go, and in doing so, we further strengthen the part of the brain that observes itself. Then, two life-changing things happen. First, we begin to truly believe that our negative feelings won't last forever. Second, this helps us become more fluid and not get stuck in feelings of anger or catastrophe, which destabilize our well-being. We become better at keeping things in perspective.

MINDFUL
ANGER MANAGEMENT
PRACTICE

I'M AS MAD AS . . .

When you are alone with your children, ask them to describe a time when they were angry or frustrated. Ask them how they reacted and how that felt. Questions will come to you, like, Were they embarrassed? Did they get angry or cry? Were they sad? Did something frighten them? Share ways of how they might have responded differently or better.

> Venting to reduce anger is like using gasoline to put out a fire—it only feeds the flame. By fueling aggressive thoughts and feelings, venting also increases aggressive responding.
>
> —Brad Bushman, PhD

THE TRAFFIC SIGNAL GAME

Remind your kids about the Guard Dog in their brains and how it gets upset. Tell them that you are going to teach them how to calm it down with something called the Traffic Signal Game. Get some paper and crayons and draw a picture of a three-colored traffic signal. Or you could show them a picture of a traffic signal or point one out when you're in the car.

Tell them that the three colors represent three different ways they can react if they ever feel angry, sad, or afraid:

- **Red:** Stop and do some mindful breathing.

- **Yellow:** Think about all the different ways to respond.

- **Green:** Try the most mindful response and see what happens.

Ask them to think again about a time when they got really mad about something. Using the Traffic Signal Game, show them how to bring themselves down from a red light to a green light. Tell them that sometimes we get so mad that we can't even think clearly in the yellow light phase. That's when they can do things like count to ten, draw, or talk to someone about how they feel. Maybe they could go out on their bike, hit a ball, or listen to some music. Remind them that bad feelings don't last forever. And when they're on the verge of a tantrum, remind them to use the traffic signals to calm down.

Suggest that they hang up the picture of the traffic signal to remind all of you to use it whenever you need to. Agree that everyone in your family will stop and go away to calm down any-time someone says, "Red light." The signals also work as a warning system. Whenever you feel yourself losing your temper with your children, tell them, "I'm about to get mad. The red light's going to come on. You'd better stop that before it does." This way they have a chance to change their behavior. Keep practicing and incorpo-rating the game into your everyday experience.

DEALING WITH ANGER

Children can easily relate to the traffic signal imagery as part of their everyday experience. This game, adapted from a system created by Roger Weissberg, professor of psychology at Yale University, is a key tool for dealing with difficult emotions.

As expert Paul Ekman explains, "The moment we become aware is less than half a second after the emotion begins, not before." In other words, we're already in the grip of a strong feeling before we know we are. It's easy for children to see themselves as victims, saying, "He made me do it" or "It wasn't my fault" or "She started it." The Traffic Signal system helps children take responsibility for their choices in response to their feelings.

> Whenever anybody loses it in our house now, one of us cries, "Red light!" and everyone has to stop shouting and go somewhere quiet to think about what just happened. It doesn't always work, but it's better than it was before.
>
> —Carla M., a MindUP parent

When we teach our children to think about the red, yellow, and green light stages of anger, it also teaches us parents to stop and think. Applying the imagery to our own anger helps to lengthen the time between impulse and action as soon as we recognize the difficult feelings. According to a study from the Department of Psychology at Virginia Tech, chronic negative reaction is one of the most consistent factors leading to child abuse, which, in turn, reinforces adverse behavior in children.

In stopping our reactivity and using our powers of reasoning, we activate the prefrontal cortex and inhibit the amygdala, so the yellow light stage will actually reduce the experience of the difficult feeling. Just thinking about ways to deal with a tricky situation helps to calm and soothe. And because of brain plasticity, we can get better at it no matter how strong our negative emotions are. The more we practice, the more we alter our brain's structure to function at its best.

The brain is an integrated whole, with strong connections between the emotional centers and the intellectual ones. This means that every time we help our children practice these mindful responses, we're not only strengthening their ability to do them but also helping them academically. What we really want for them beyond any school success, though, is to build their emotional resilience—to get up when they fall.

> *For the first time my son has been able to manage his anger much better. And his empathy has grown. But the greatest thing is that for the first time in his life, he put his arms around me and told me he loved me.*
>
> —Laura C., a MindUP parent

Sadness

There are as many nights as days, and the one is just as long as the other. . . . Even a happy life cannot be without a measure of darkness.

—Carl Jung

Sadness can be extremely challenging for children. One of the reasons is that most are more embarrassed by their tears than by their anger. Boys in particular see crying as a sign of weakness.

However, it's perfectly normal and even healthy to feel sad. We just need to learn how to handle it. Dark days can follow if we don't become fully aware. We need to find ways to grow from our down moments instead of developing a victim mentality.

It's healthier to help ourselves out of darkness by talking, sharing, and communicating our feelings. How we handle our own sadness is key to how our children will handle theirs.

Do we show or hide our feelings? Are we in denial of our sadness? Do we share our feelings with our children? The latest research on emotional intelligence shows that when people understand their feelings and are able to share them appropriately, they have healthier friendships, better connections with those they work with, and stronger personal relationships. This honesty is an antidote to depression or a sense of isolation.

Children are no different. Sharing truths with them is important. Sharing keeps us all happier and healthier and takes away the loneliness of sadness. We are a beacon of light in their lives, and we help inform them of the best way to deal with their emotions.

Support your children's feelings no matter how small; they are not small to them. I have heard parents sometimes becoming impatient and saying, "Stop crying!" or "I'm fed up with you moping around!" Some parents seem to have an aversion to crying children. I once knew a father who couldn't handle tears, whether they were shed during a sad movie or caused by a scrape on the knee. He made his child feel stupid for weeping. I was horrified. How alone and confused that little person must have felt.

> *Children experiencing loss need to feel free to openly express their feelings of sadness and grief. Be careful to avoid minimizing their feelings.*
>
> —National Network for Child Care

Children need to know that feeling these emotions is as natural as anything else, like laughing, sleeping, eating, or playing. It's good to share these feelings together—it gives our children support.

Reflections

I was one of ten children chosen to hold the end of a ribbon in the maypole dance. I was in third grade. I was proud of being a dancer and knew how to follow directions. I could really dance the dance. I swept the ribbon over and under and over and under, building a beautiful braid at the top of the pole. It was a cinch. Out of my reverie I heard my teacher yell out, "Stop! Goldie, you have made a mistake!" I felt like she was spitting on me as she said, "You went under too many times, and now we have to start all over again!" I was horrified. It was my fault that every student had to go back, retracing their steps to our starting position. The corners of my mouth dipped down involuntarily. I couldn't control my tears and they began to flow. I was so embarrassed to cry in front of everyone. I felt misunderstood and ashamed; I had been so confident that I was doing my very best. I have never forgotten the feeling.

It is important to remember that when children are sad it can be about things that we adults are not affected by—the death of a goldfish, the loss of a favorite toy, or not being picked for the sports team. They might have been teased at school or made a mistake that embarrassed them in front of their friends.

Children don't always open up and share their sad feelings with us, which sometimes makes it a challenge for us to help them. Rather than telling them not to feel sad, it is better to acknowledge their feelings.

In their book *Emotionally Intelligent Parenting*, educational psychologists Maurice Elias, Steven Tobias, and Brian Friedlander suggest ways of prompting reluctant children into saying what is on their minds. These include saying things like, "It seems as if something may be bothering you today. You aren't acting like you usually do, and I'd like to talk to you about that." Once we find out what the problem is, we need to thank them for telling us how they feel and acknowledge that it makes sense to feel that way by saying something like, "Yes, that must feel bad. I remember when something similar happened to me and I felt sad, too, but we can't expect to feel happy all the time."

When we do this, we attune to our children, which allows them to feel seen and heard by us. Such attunement also gives children the sense that they have done something good and helps their brains regulate emotion and relate to it in a healthy way. Having their feelings received may be all they need. If they remain sad, researchers say distraction is the best course of action.

Sadness is a natural reaction to painful circumstances. However, experiencing sadness over a prolonged period of time will lead to depression. It is important to revisit the dangers of letting sadness and grief fester and become habituated. Depression has far deeper symptoms and may not even be tied to something painful happening. It can also linger for months or years.

Professor Mark Williams, a clinical psychologist at Oxford University, found that those who can't snap out of their depression get stuck in what he calls "adhesive preoccupation" by reacting to sad events with a fretful cycle of negative or brooding thoughts. According to the AACAP, any of the following symptoms may mean that a child is depressed rather than just sad:

- Frequent displays of sadness, tearfulness, or crying

- Expressions of hopelessness

- Decreased interest in activities or inability to enjoy previously favorite activities

- Persistent boredom; low energy

- Social isolation; poor communication

- Low self-esteem and guilt

- Extreme sensitivity to rejection or failure

- Increased irritability, anger, or hostility

- Difficulty with relationships

- Frequent complaints of physical illnesses, such as headaches and stomachaches

- Frequent absences from school or poor performance in school

- Poor concentration

- A major change in eating or sleeping patterns

- Talk of running away or efforts to run away from home

- Thoughts or expressions of suicide or self-destructive behavior

If ever we are worried about our child's emotional well-being or our own, we need to seek professional help. And we also need to remember that seeking such help doesn't mean we've failed or that we'll be judged in some way.

Research has found that many parents, especially those who are better-off and more concerned with what their friends and neighbors think, tend to either ignore or try to manage emotional problems in their children rather than face any kind of social stigma. This can be counterproductive for everyone concerned.

Reflections

The saddest times in my life were when I lost my parents. When my father died, I still had my mother, but when I lost her, I was an orphan who knew that no one would ever love me like that again because I'd lost a very special kind of love. But I was also a mother and a wife, and I knew I had to bring myself back to a place where I could feel happy again and be present joyfully for my family. It was very difficult to pull myself out of such deep sadness and try to generate more joy. The whole process took about six months. To help, I read books that I hoped would give me a sense of future, instead of longing for something that I couldn't have any longer. I also shared how I was feeling with my children because I knew, from my own childhood experience, that sadness can be catching. I let them know that I was still me but that I was feeling sad because I lost my mother. I told them sadness was something that we all experience and that it's important to be sad whenever we suffer loss. Because I'm such a naturally joyful person, whenever I am sad people always try to shift me out of my sorrow, trying to cajole me into a better state of mind. I appreciate their concern, but I have come to learn that going through those periods of sadness are vitally important to my growth and to my inner relationship with myself. I have never run from sadness or sorrow. I live within it for a while, but I'm always careful not to stay in it for very long.

Many parents feel at a loss when it comes to talking to children about death and other tragedies. We don't want to scare them about the hard stuff or make them feel sad unnecessarily. And yet, how do we help them when something tragic touches their lives?

Therapists advise that we should explain that everyone has tough events to cope with but that each time a hard thing happens, it's a chance to grow our hearts and be kind to one another. Then we can share with them what our most difficult time was, or how a friend or relative had a sad thing happen once. These conversations will help our children integrate their sadness, recognize that they are not alone, and accept that the tough stuff is part of life that we all grow past.

MINDFUL
SADNESS MANAGEMENT
PRACTICE

Whenever your children are feeling sad about something, sit somewhere quietly with them and ask them how they are feeling. Do they want to cry? Would they prefer to be on their own? Do they feel all churned up inside?

Tell them how you feel when you're sad and explain that crying is one of the natural responses to sadness. Reassure them that it's perfectly okay to cry and that they won't feel sad forever. Tell them they can go somewhere private if they feel embarrassed about crying in public.

STORYTELLING

Read your children a story in which a character feels sad about something or talk about a recent film you might have seen together in which something sad happened. Explain that when something upsetting happens or someone they love dies, they might feel sad for a long time. Tell them that this is normal, and that it is also normal to laugh and feel happy during times of sadness. Point out that no matter how sad they might feel about something, in time these feelings will soften and change.

SHARING YOUR SADNESS

Explain what you did to make yourself feel better when you were sad. Maybe you went for a walk or bought yourself something, ate ice cream, or went to the movies to see a happy film. Maybe you sat and thought of happier times.

LOOK AT YOUR HAPPY WALL

Ask your children what they can do to make themselves feel better if they feel sad. Maybe come up with a list of things they could try so they can use it if they need to. For instance, they might like a hug, to talk to an understanding person, to watch a happy movie, or to bake cookies. If you made a Happy Wall (from chapter 10, "Happiness"), spend some time with it. If you didn't, this might be a good time to create one.

TRAFFIC SIGNAL GAME

Remind your children of the Traffic Signal Game and tell them they can also use it when they're sad. *Red:* Stop. *Yellow:* Think of distracting or comforting things to do. *Green:* Try doing one.

WHAT DOES SADNESS LOOK LIKE?

Ask your children to draw what sadness feels like in their bodies. What color is it? Blue, maybe? Or black? Afterward, talk about what images and sensations came up. How can they tell when someone else is sad? How does it show on people's faces or in their body language? Can they tell from how people speak? Help them understand that sadness is natural and that they can soothe themselves whenever they feel sad.

OVERCOMING SADNESS, ACCEPTING CHANGE

Children are partly dominated by "magical thinking," where they experience themselves at the center of things. Therefore they may believe that their thoughts, feelings, wishes, and actions can cause what happens to them and others. . . . Such thinking can make a child think that he or she caused [a] death.

—Atle Dyregrov, PhD

The events that make us sad are often those that also lead to change, and change is what shapes the universe. People fear change, especially children who crave stability and routine, but change can be good.

Change shakes us from complacency and makes us sit up and take notice. It helps us focus on what is good and important in our lives. Change stops us from stagnating and, in opening us up to other possibilities, leads to transformation.

By teaching children how they can deal with change or overcome the obstacles they'll face in their lives, we give them one of the most valuable tools they can have in their armory against the sad times they will undoubtedly experience.

Divorce: The Hardest Change

The breakup of a marriage or similar relationship is hard on adults as well as children. When we fall in love, we expect it to be forever. All our emotional hopes and dreams are rolled up into one person, who promises many things that can't always be delivered.

Sadly, our dreams don't always come true. It's hard enough when it happens, but when children are involved it becomes doubly tough. Your biggest fear is that your offspring will become the spoils of divorce and that the breakup will cause them pain.

There are no clear-cut answers on how to deal with this situation. Emotions run high: jealousy, anger, resentment, and sadness. To be fully aware and present at this difficult time is a challenge, but mindful practice can help immensely in regulating your most negative and destructive emotions. Using your breathing can stop reactive responses every time your buttons get pushed.

Frankly, this subject is worthy of an entire book. But I wanted to shed some light on the universal problem of how to get along with your ex-spouse or ex-partner for the sake of your children. Lawyers sometimes refer to the children of divorce as "soft bullets," as they are often deployed as ammunition in an ongoing war.

Our children suffer the most whenever anger hijacks our better thinking. The breakup of their family is the most traumatic event in their young lives. They have no idea how to handle these raging emotions. In all their worst nightmares, they never considered the possibility that they might end up without their parents. They feel responsible, helpless, and guilty. We may think they're coping because they are young and seem resilient, but the symptoms of their anxiety will start to emerge: bed-wetting, an inability to sleep, temper tantrums, or a general feeling of malaise.

The simplest yet often hardest answer is first to deal with your own anger because that alone can poison your child's emotional life. Remind yourself of some or all of the lessons you have learned, such as mindful breathing and mindful listening. Remember about keeping perspective and forgiveness. Try to make these qualities a daily practice to develop some sort of emotional stability.

Put your children first. Please don't speak badly about your ex-spouse to them. Don't forget that their parents are theirs for life and will always be their first loves. Your children will learn to appreciate the ways and truths of adult relationships in time, but they will never stop loving their parents.

Try to practice gratitude. Remember the good times. Focus on the reason you were with your ex in the first place. However it ended, your relationship gave you your beautiful children. Remind yourself of all the good things about your ex, and be sure to demonstrate your support in front of your children. Keep in mind that in time things will change. Emotions will settle, and you may even find yourself part of a new, blended family. Hopefully you will have dealt with your resentment skillfully, and you can be empathetic, kind, and gracious when those challenges arise. And, believe me, they will. . . .

Try to remember that every cause for sadness has some hidden treasure in it to be excavated for future use. Diamonds reveal themselves out of dirt. Lotus flowers spring from the mud. Recognizing that and embracing the feelings that go with change make us stronger and better able to face the future with courage and optimism.

Fear

We must build dikes of courage to hold back the flood of fear.
—Martin Luther King Jr.

When I was a child, I was afraid of the dark and had to have my mother rub my back until I fell asleep. When I felt her get up from the bed to leave, I'd call out, "Please come back, Mommy, and rub me some more." She always came back and never left me feeling afraid.

Life can be incredibly scary to a child. There is so much activity going on in their brains that we are sometimes left playing a guessing game as to why they have become fearful—as with night terrors in toddlers. It is so frightening to watch our babies become confused, distressed, and lose control in the middle of the night. We feel so helpless.

Some children are hardwired to worry, according to Jerome Kagan, a pioneer in developmental psychology at Harvard University. After studying the temperaments of people from infancy to adulthood, he discovered that up to 20 percent of babies are "high-reactive," or more strongly fearful, from the day they're born. These children grow up to be inhibited, anxious, and fearful adults.

Of all the emotions, fear is the one most strongly activated by the amygdala. It is constantly scanning the environment for problems or threats of any kind, ready to turn on the stress response.

If you think your child may fall into that category, don't worry; you can make a difference. The good news is that learning tech-

> *Fear tends to overrule reason, as the amygdala hobbles our logic and reasoning circuits. That makes fear far, far more powerful than reason. It evolved as a mechanism to protect us from life-threatening situations, and from an evolutionary standpoint there's nothing more important than that.*
>
> —Michael Fanselow

niques to calm anxiety can help. And the younger they start, the better. Research shows that anxious children who learn good coping skills to deal with their fear are less likely to develop anxiety disorders as adults.

It is well noted that anger is only fear in disguise. Take notice next time and see if the things we're frightened of or defensive about often make us angry.

Have you ever experienced anger when your child runs out into the street to retrieve a ball without thinking? I can remember my mother getting so angry when I would fall and hurt myself. It made me cry even more, not understanding that she was afraid for my well-being. I thought

> *The distraction technique worked so well whenever my children were upset or frightened that I decided to try it for myself. The next time my son went out on his bike, instead of waiting by the window watching for his return, I went and planted some flowers. When he came back, I was elbow-deep in earth and had almost forgotten that I'd been worried.*
>
> —A MindUP mom

she was mad at me. I, too, experienced anger like that with my little one when she let go of my hand to go back into the street to pick up a toy she had dropped. Our responses have great impact. Managing them is challenging and difficult. However, when we take ourselves off automatic response we can manage our outcomes so much better.

MINDFUL

FEAR MANAGEMENT

PRACTICE

MINDFUL BREATHING AND FEELING

Whenever your children are afraid, find a quiet place to sit with them and practice some mindful breathing together. Ask them what it feels like in their bodies. What are the sensations? What color are they? Are they growing or calming down? Do some more breathing together for a few minutes and notice what happens to those sensations. Ask them how they feel now.

Remind them of the workings of their own brains and that fear is just a response to the amygdala firing up. The Guard Dog has been let out of his pen and is barking again! Refresh their memories about how, by using their breathing, they can shut it back in and calm down and think straight again.

Talk about something they used to be afraid of or worried about: for instance, learning to swim or ride a bike, their first game with a new sports team, or their first day at school. Ask them how they coped with their feelings. Help them remember that they got through the experience and that their fears were temporary. Be sure to resonate with your child's feelings and show empathy and caring. You might say something like, "You're scared. That's natural. I'm sorry you're afraid. I remember when I felt like that when I was young, too."

THE TRAFFIC SIGNAL GAME

Use the Traffic Signal Game for fear. *Red:* Stop and sit quietly. *Yellow:* Think about things to do that will help, like mindful breathing or talking to a grown-up. *Green:* Pick one of those things to try.

CHANGING THE CHANNEL

One of the best ways to defuse fear is to distract the brain from habituating such thoughts over and over again. Tell them it's just like changing the channel on the TV from a scary movie to a happy cartoon. You might say, "Let's go feed the ducks in the park," or suggest some other fun activity. It's important to both empathize with their feelings *and* help them change the subject, striking the right balance.

SOLVING THE PROBLEM

Have a problem-solving quiz. Ask questions like, "Mindy is afraid of dogs, but she really wants to go over to the house of a friend who has a large dog. What should she do?" or "John is frightened about a spelling test tomorrow. What can he do?"

Let your children know that they can come to you whenever they get scared. This is a wonderful way to create connectivity with your child. When you have finished, do some mindful breathing together so that you end in a calm place.

* * *

There's a particular kind of fear that only parents feel—and that, of course, is fear for our children. These days, parental fears go far deeper than the age-old concerns about them walking to school, learning to drive, or going out on dates. Our world has changed, and the new challenges have hit our children hard. The future for our kids looks uncertain in many ways—for example, when we realize how far in debt they may already be before they leave college. A sense of hopelessness and apathy can envelop them. The stresses they feel are palpable. We would like to say it's all going to be okay, but we are in the dark sometimes as well when it comes to understanding the solutions it takes to create change. This is why I believe the mindfulness techniques I have been outlining are so very important. These practices build inner resiliency and self-awareness, essential traits for an individual to survive and succeed. Starting at home with the development of these skills is part of the solution.

Reflections

When our children were young, Kurt and I were careful not to be away at the same time so that one of us would always be home to give a sense of security and safety. Once they were a little older, however, we decided to go to Turkey for a vacation. The two of us were having a wonderful time in Istanbul when we received a call that there had been an earthquake in Los Angeles. We called home immediately and told our children we were coming back. When we arrived the next day, they were still very frightened. They were afraid to go to school and afraid to go to sleep. Kurt and I decided to nestle down together with them for a few days. We didn't go out. We ate together. We tucked each of them into bed at night. The combination of the earthquake and us being away had made a very deep imprint on their brains. We had to create more familial, positive experiences to offset the negatives so that the incident could exist in their minds as a memory of bonding family time and not be triggered repeatedly as a trauma. It took a few days, but things soon returned to normal.

FROM FEAR AND ANXIETY TO COOL AND CALM

Fear and anxiety can be caused by anything from a school test to a new job, a military deployment, or a sporting challenge. Whatever the cause, mindfulness techniques are an invaluable tool for those about to experience extreme stress.

Mindfulness training has been proven to help people in all sorts of ways, but one study found that when given to U.S. Marines about to be deployed to Iraq, it helped protect them against functional impairments associated with high-stress challenges.

> *Anxiety is . . . a kind of fear gone wild, a generalized sense of dread about something out there that seems menacing—but that in truth is not menacing, and may not even be out there. If you're anxious, you find it difficult to talk yourself out of this foreboding; you become trapped in an endless loop of what-ifs.*
>
> —Robin Marantz Henig

A study by Amishi Jha, then at the University of Pennsylvania, and Elizabeth A. Stanley of Georgetown University highlighted ways of tackling such emotional reactivity. "Our findings suggest that—just as daily physical exercise leads to physical fitness—engaging in mindfulness exercises on a regular basis may improve mind-fitness," reports Professor Jha. "Working memory is an important feature of mind-fitness. Not only does it safeguard against distraction and emotional reactivity, but it also provides a mental workspace to ensure quick-and-considered decisions and action plans. Building mind-fitness with mindfulness training may help anyone who must maintain peak performance in the face of extremely stressful circumstances."

With the increasing rate of post-traumatic stress disorder and other mental health issues experienced by those returning from war, offering mindfulness training prior to deployment may buffer against potential lifelong psychological illness. If it can help fully grown men cope with the stress of such extreme situations, imagine what it could do for children facing challenges at home or at school that make them equally fearful.

Anxiety is another big issue for children, and this often comes from repressed fear or from anger that they haven't been able to express. When we keep our feelings to ourselves for any length of time, we can develop symptoms of anxiety and not really know why we feel scared or panicked.

I had my own intimate relationship with anxiety when I was younger, and I can honestly say it was the scariest thing I'd ever experienced. I developed full-blown panic attacks in which I felt there were no walls to hold on to anymore. I was alone. My heart pounded uncontrollably. I became dizzy in public places. I felt sick to my stomach. I functioned, but only with incredible fear inside. I would go home and sit in my chair and knit, and it was the only place I felt safe.

In exploring what was happening to me, I found that my anxiety arose through self-preservation. I'd been repressing angry feelings I had toward my partner. I was afraid that he wouldn't like me anymore if I expressed them, and so they festered. I was also afraid for my future. I'd been plucked from the safety of the chorus line to a place alone in the spotlight, which was never part of my life plan. When you are taken out of your comfort zone and all your expectations change, it can be the most frightening and destabilizing event of your life.

As parents, we need to remember that moving to a new house, changing our relationships, shifting jobs, or switching schools can be extremely unsettling to a child. Just as in an earthquake, they feel they have no firm ground to stand on anymore. They feel vulnerable, frightened, and confused. They need to know that however violent the shift, they still have you to cling to, which is why it's so vital to establish secure attachment when they are very young.

Empathy

*A human being . . . experiences himself, his thoughts, and
feelings as something separated from the rest—a kind of
optical delusion of his consciousness. This delusion is a kind
of prison for us. . . . Our task must be to free ourselves from
this prison by widening our circles of compassion to embrace
all living creatures and the whole of nature in its beauty.*

—Albert Einstein

"Before you abuse, criticize, and accuse, then walk a mile in my
shoes." What a lyric that was that Elvis sang to us—and how true.

Every day, life presents us with opportunities to be compassionate, feel someone else's sadness or pain, and see things from
another person's point of view. Sometimes we just think about
doing those things and don't follow through. Whenever we do
reach out to someone, though, it can be the greatest feeling in the
world. It's good to know that we are somewhat hardwired to feel
empathy, even though some people are less available emotionally
to feel the pain of others. The good news is, they can become
more compassionate if they wish. Anyone can practice empathy
by doing the following:

- Develop better listening skills.

- Put yourself in someone else's shoes.

- Practice forgiving even your worst enemy.

- Practice gratitude and show appreciation for even the small gifts of others.

Our children are especially open to being taught these attributes. This is particularly true from the age of four. From this point on they have the ability to appreciate that other people may have different beliefs from their own. We can actively help them develop this by attuning to others and becoming more connected and sensitized to other people's needs.

I'm not proposing we all sit around the fire and sing "Kumbaya." But the benefits and powers gained from demonstrating empathy are too good to miss. It creates greater intimacy in partnerships. It helps us become in tune with our life. Empathy can also be a precursor to forgiveness, which is one of the most important acts of all. To forgive is a very hard thing to do, but once we do it, our whole perspective changes. Something profound happens in our brains when we forgive. It has been scientifically proven to be beneficial. And when your children see you in an act of forgiveness, they will embody the same quality.

Caring and empathy are necessary to build a healthy society. Today our children are becoming more and more desensitized, and empathy is being forsaken. The constant exposure to violence in various streams of media and games becomes a "game changer" in itself by rewiring parts of the brain.

Young brains have the capacity for all these actions, but they need to see us model these behaviors first. They then need to practice themselves in order for their brains to wire up with these particular aspects of emotional intelligence.

Knowing how to get along with others gives children a feeling of success and a sense of being in control. It also prepares them for the future. So much depends on our ability to work and play productively with other people and see all sides of a situation.

How intelligent we are or what our IQ is has nothing to do with how compassionate or empathetic we are, and vice versa. These are two different parts of the brain at work. But to strengthen our EQ, balance is necessary. If you can give your children a direct emotional link to empathy, they'll connect with that and remember it.

You can help build your children's direct experience with feeling empathy by taking them with you if you are going to do anything related to charitable giving, such as taking toys to underprivileged children or visiting elders in a retirement home or sick kids in the hospital. Creating compassion in this way enhances their ability to develop a healthy communion with those around them. It also helps them see things from other people's perspective. Only when they pull away emotionally from a problem they may be having with someone and view it from a distance can they start to resolve it without the charge of strong emotions like anger or resentment.

William Ury, from Harvard's Program on Negotiation, calls this distancing "going to the balcony." This metaphor describes the emotional disconnect we need to foster instead of always reacting to conflicts. Instead of being stuck in the drama of a situation, we imagine being on the balcony in a movie theater watching it like a film. From that distance, we can see the whole

picture and then find better solutions. Psychologist Martin Seligman describes perspective taking as "seeing into the soul."

For us as parents, this ability is also crucially important because it allows us to better understand our children. By pulling
away from the issues that stick in our craw, we can look at a situation dispassionately and with a more refined view and then respond more skillfully. Sometimes when we do that, it actually
makes us feel more compassionate and empathetic. It stimulates
these responses because we are no longer attached to our negative emotions.

Helping our children develop this ability to understand their
own minds is critical to their emotional well-being. It helps
not only with their social development but also with their self-
awareness. With greater objectivity it becomes easier to solve
problems and use their powers of critical thinking. So when, for
example, your son is upset because a friend has taken something
of his, you could say something like this:

> Okay, now let's play the Balcony Game. Why don't we "go to the
> balcony" and look at this situation as though it's a story? Let's
> come up with two different names. How about Johnny and Greg?
> Johnny took a car from Greg's toy box, and Greg is very upset. It's
> his car, and he wants it back. Why do you think he wants his car
> back so badly? Does he have any other toys to play with? Does
> Johnny? What do you think would be a good thing to do? How
> about if Greg lets Johnny play with his car until he's bored? What
> could Greg play with instead? Maybe his plane?

This kind of game can be adapted to many different situations. It helps your children negotiate their way through an ex-

perience without taking things so personally, and then make informed decisions. This is because in order to empathize with how others are thinking and feeling, they first have to recognize their own thoughts and feelings. It becomes a reinforcing cycle: Understanding and being patient with our own minds helps us understand and be patient with the minds of others. Understanding others helps us understand ourselves.

When we develop this capacity in ourselves and teach it to our children, we build a stronger family that understands and respects differences in thoughts, emotions, and motivations of all family members. If our children see that we parents can deal positively with our negative feelings, then they realize they can as well.

Perspective taking is also good for our children's brains because it helps build the necessary circuitry to calm anxiety, exercise impulse control, and foresee the possible outcomes of actions. In a sense, it gives children the keys to their own minds. Only then are they able to make better choices rather than simply acting on impulse—such as when they lash out at a friend.

It also helps them academically because it builds the brain's ability to interpret new information, use stored knowledge, and predict the right answer. In other words, as they learn to consider various points of view, it actually develops the part of the brain that considers all the options. For instance, on tests they can pick the best answer. This ability also protects them from making dangerous choices.

There are various complex parts of the brain that have to operate well together to practice empathy. As parents, we can help this brain integration by talking to our children in ways that increase their understanding of themselves and others. Without these crucial conversations, the circuitry may not get fully wired up properly.

In teaching empathy, it is also important that we show respect for our children's thoughts and feelings, no matter how hard that may be. Jon Kabat-Zinn, PhD, calls it "soul recognition." He adds, "We need to trust the sovereignty and intrinsic beauty and goodness we are born with and encourage our children to be who they are." Respecting our children's feelings doesn't mean letting them have their way all the time, and we certainly don't have to agree with their thoughts or feelings.

Reflections

Many years ago I attended a scientific conference hosted by the Mind & Life Institute in Dharamsala, India, and took Boston and Oliver with me. We visited the Tibetan Children's Village, a Montessori school for children, some of whom had parents and some of whom did not. I had longed to go there after many visits to Dharamsala, and what a blessing that I had two of my sons with me. We mounted the stairs to the toddlers' section, where the housemother placed a fourteen-month-old boy wearing pink fuzzy feet pajamas in my arms. What a beautiful boy. He seemed so calm. The housemother said he had just arrived from the hospital. His name was Tensin. He was left on a doorstep with a note that said his mother had died at birth and his father could no longer care for him. I didn't want to let him go. We were all drawn to his energy and sweetness, and the boys played with him, too. I put Tensin down for his tea break with the other children. We had to leave. I thought I would sneak away while he was being distracted by his cookies and warm tea. I peeked behind the bushes for a last glance. He got up all by himself, turned in our direction, looked around for us, and started walking right toward us. We were in love. The following day I went back with the boys, and again the day after that. Tensin is now twelve years old, and I have stayed in close contact over the years, visiting him every so often. I hadn't been there in several years, and the last time I went my heart was pounding as I ran up the steps of the home to see him again. There he was with the same curious smile and dancing eyes, dressed in the clothes I had sent him. I ran over to him and hugged him hard. He put his arms around me and giggled shyly into my chest. Our loving connection was still so strong. We spent the day together, and although his English wasn't great and my Tibetan is very limited, it didn't matter. That wonderful part of us that communicates nonverbally went to work. Our day together was just about perfect. With caring and compassion, my hope for Tensin is that he grows to be a happy, healthy young man who feels of value to his society. And I hope we will be friends forever.

MINDFUL
EMPATHY
PRACTICE

HOW ARE THEY FEELING?

Whenever you pass by someone on the street or in another car, play a game with your children that starts with, "I wonder what that person is feeling?" Be as creative and inventive as you like. Does the person look happy or sad? Is the person frowning or smiling? Label those emotions: anger, joy, sadness . . . Talk about

> *The power of empathy and acceptance is immense and deeply transformative for both sides.*
>
> —Jon Kabat-Zinn, PhD

how we can tell what someone's feeling just by looking at them. Explain that sensing what someone else is feeling is empathy. Encourage your kids to share their feelings, too.

DRAWING FROM A NEW POINT OF VIEW

Whenever you are sitting quietly with your children, pull out some paper and crayons and find a piece of fruit or other handy object. Place it on a table and suggest that each of you draw it. Then switch to the other side of the table or room and draw the object again. What are the differences between the two drawings? What is the same—the shape and the color? Does it change when drawn from the other side?

MAKING A NEST

Find a toy or favorite object and bring it to your child, or buy something specially. Tell him that you are going to sit together and make a nest for the toy. Use anything from tissue paper or scraps of material to torn-up strips of newspaper or a cardboard box. Help your child create the nest, a place where it can always be safe from harm. Encourage him to make the nest comfortable and keep it somewhere dry and warm. Teach him to take care of his toy and check on it every so often. This caretaking skill will help him appreciate needs other than his own with love and respect.

SMALL AND TALL

The next game can be played whenever you are having fun goofing around with your children. Tell them it's called Small and Tall. Begin by all of you crawling on your hands and knees pretending to be cats or dogs. Have some fun with it and make noises. Then stand on chairs and look at everything as if you were as tall as giraffes. Afterward, ask what was different between the two viewpoints. What could they see from one position that they couldn't see from the other? Explain that whether they are on the floor or standing on a chair, there is not right or wrong; there are only differences.

Have your child pick one of her favorite stories. Compare the different characters. Talk about what each was thinking and feeling. Did they have different points of view? Ask her which side she agrees with and whether she can understand how the other side feels.

BEING EMPATHETIC

Practicing empathy is being *tuned in* and *in tune* to the inner worlds of others and making an emotional connection to that.

It creates a greater capacity for tolerance, which diminishes the differences between us. We think beyond our own wants and needs and become curious about other people's. Empathy stops us from being selfish.

In the past few years, research on empathy has suggested that it is key—if not *the* key—to all human social interaction and morality. Without empathy we wouldn't have a conscience. Empathy engenders trust, social cohesion, and honesty.

In ancient Greece, the Spartans and the Athenians raised their children very differently. The people of Sparta were a warrior race who brought up their young boys in an environment of brutality. To encourage ruthlessness they starved them so that they would steal food from other boys

> A pupil named Andrew was crying. One of his friends brought him to the center of the classroom, and the rest of the kids listened when Andrew explained that he wasn't going to see his father for three months. One told him not to feel sad and that they'd all help. Another said it was okay to be sad but not to worry—as time passed it would get easier. He then spoke of what happened when his dad had cancer and was in the hospital for three months. Another child said how much he missed his father after his parents divorced. Finally, another boy said quietly that he last saw his dad when he was four, and he wouldn't get to see him for a long time because he was in prison. All this took place in a matter of five minutes—the most meaningful minutes of my teaching career.
>
> —Carolyn J., a MindUP teacher

and learn to be devious. They were, in fact, trained to be killers. In Athens, on the other hand, children were nurtured in the home.

They learned music, poetry, and art at a young age. When they grew up, they became pioneers of culture, democracy, and the arts.

Psychologists say that we can teach our children to be Athenians or Spartans. We might not train our children to be assassins in such a brutal way in modern society, but unless we teach them the importance of empathy for others, they will be poorly equipped when it comes to anything from clashes in the playground to unexpected changes in the home.

By knowing and trusting in our goodness, we can free ourselves to share that goodness with others. Then we create a ripple effect emanating from our good deeds, spreading even more empathy and joy. This unwritten code of conduct reflects our true selves and feeds our inner souls. It is our way of reaching out from our hearts and touching the hearts of others.

BULLYING

Preschool years are a prime time for setting a foundation for building empathy. A child who has been taught empathetic behavior will have much more emotional regulation during his or her school years. It's wonderful how all these different aspects of mindfulness connect to give our children healthier and happier futures.

Empathy also plays a vital role in preventing bullying, which is endemic in our schools. At least 25 percent of students report being bullied every day, according to the Department of Education. The figure could be much higher. What researchers at Yale University call "bullycide" is on the rise, with increasing numbers of desperate children committing suicide because of the way their fellow pupils treat them.

Antibullying initiatives like telephone hotlines and class therapy help, but the development of empathy is the one that most educators are currently focusing on. This is because it can help children see the bigger picture. If we can teach them perspective, we hope that, in time, they will learn how not to act solely out of self-interest. Children are affected so deeply by cruelty, and they take it so personally. I have heard some of the most horrible stories from parents, tales that bring tears to my eyes. I have also heard amazing success stories from parents who've shared how MindUP changed their bullied child's world and how they now look forward to going to school. Empathy practice can help children be more resilient in the face of slings and arrows.

If you help your children develop empathetic skills at an early age, chances are they won't grow into bullies as adolescents and will instead defend the underdogs. This is especially important, as figures show that bullying is most common in middle and high schools. Children who develop empathy have been found to be 64 percent more likely to step in and intervene if they witness bullying and to defend vulnerable children. When a sense of community is engendered like this, it can quite literally change lives.

In one program, called Roots of Empathy, which started in Canada, young mothers and their babies visit classrooms regularly, and the children discuss their responses to the baby's emotions. If it smiles, they talk about that. If it cries, they consider what might be bothering the baby and how to make things better. Students are taught that a crying baby isn't a bad baby; it's just a baby with a problem that it can't express. They learn to put themselves in the baby's shoes and feel its frustration. When we lay this kind of foundation of caring, empathetic people can create a culture shift.

BLENDED FAMILIES: SPECIAL OPPORTUNITIES FOR PRACTICING EMPATHY

There can be few greater challenges to family life than the blended family. Just when you have recovered from the fallout from a divorce, something else comes along that will require all your strength, patience, and wisdom.

It might be you that has to adjust to the arrival of a new stepchild or the child that has to adjust to you. Feelings will still be raw. Blame may be laid. Children angry at the changes forced upon them may act out, and you may become the target. All children want to believe that their parents will get back together. The new family they are expected to accept represents the end of that dream. There will be a lot of secret hurt.

On top of all that additional sadness, your children may suddenly find themselves with new siblings or a new stepmom or stepdad. There will be so many adjustments to be made, both physical and emotional. Bedrooms may have to be shared. A house move or switch of schools might be necessary. Previous family routines and traditions will be interrupted. Resentment and frustration will abound. Your children will feel as if everything is out of their control.

What is needed here is a large dose of empathy. It will act like a salve on the problems of a blended family. Keep the lines of communication open. Allow everyone involved to be heard and understood even if you disagree with them. Try to inject some fun into the situation. Look for the positives. Try to distract children from getting stuck in a loop about something. If you have a problem, you can say things like, "We know how hard this is, and we respect your feelings. This is new for all of us, and we're in it together. But this is where we are now, so let's figure it out and try to have a good time."

The most important thing is to listen to your children and react with empathy as you discuss these difficult transitional times. They feel displaced and destabilized. They'll be afraid that they'll lose you to the other children or your new partner. Their loyalties will switch back and forth, and sometimes they'll try to manipulate the situation. Be aware. Be mindful and use your skills to tune in and respond skillfully. Keep calm. Let your children guide you and lead the way. Don't try to force issues. Imagine what it would be like to be them in this situation and show compassion. Give them all your support and love.

Put your mindful breathing practices to work to help defuse issues of anger and fear. There will never be a better time than that provided by this kind of drama to make them stop, sit, and breathe. Build a firm foundation of trust, honesty, and caring. Your children have found themselves in the middle, with responsibilities they didn't ask for. It's important to take the load off their shoulders and assume the responsibility of skillfully managing your relationships. Sometimes working with ex-partners and their new partners can be very hard. But this is the benefit of putting yourself in someone else's shoes. Using empathy to put aside your differences is the high road worth taking.

In the words of John Kehoe, speaker, teacher, and author, empathy is everything. He writes, "You [can] help change the vibration of the whole human species. It is not just the acts you perform that change the world . . . it is the change in you that changes the world. For every person who lives an authentic life, whatever that may look like, thousands if not millions will be affected without ever meeting or knowing that person. What awesome possibilities this presents to each of us. Life is forever calling to us to be authentic and giving us experiences to live an authentic life through our actions."

Kindness

Be kind, for everyone you meet is fighting a hard battle.

—Plato

Kindness comes from thoughtfulness. Having empathized with someone and seen things from his or her perspective, we take it one stage further and do something kind that lets the person know we care. Caring about someone is compassion in action.

In an ideal world, we should all be drawn to acts of kindness whether or not we think it is good for us. Once we learn about the remarkable scientific findings on what kindness actually does to our brains, we'll be hooked.

More than thirty years ago, researchers Ellen Langer and Judith Rodin conducted a landmark study at a U.S. nursing home in which they gave each resident a potted plant. One group was asked to care for the plant themselves, and another group was told that the nurses would tend to their plant for them. Three weeks later, the researchers found that those who had taken care of their own plants reported much higher levels of happiness than those who'd let the nurses do it. Eighteen months later, fewer of those who cared for plants had died, and those who survived were more active and in better health than their fellow residents who didn't have a plant. These findings triggered a flurry of further research proving that activities ranging from having to look after a pet to doing something kind for a friend made people happier and extended their lives.

It is our mirror neurons that form the basis for this capacity for kindness and empathy. Mirror neurons act like this: If we see people smile, we feel like smiling. If they cry, we often cry, too. We mirror each other's emotions, which resonates profoundly whenever we are practicing kindness. Even watching someone being kind triggers the same physiological changes in the brain as those triggered in the person being kind. This fascinating finding led to an explosion of research that revealed that it's not just what we see physically that activates our mirror neuron circuitry but what we *imagine* is going on inside someone else. We literally feel what others are going through. From that awareness, we are moved to action.

The more we use our mirror neuron circuitry by practicing helping others, the stronger that circuitry becomes. Like exercising a muscle, we literally grow our brain's ability to care. Acts of kindness raise our own optimism, making us happier. Dopamine levels rise in the brain and activate the brain's pleasure centers, so it's a win-win situation—and a wonderful way of getting out of a depressed state, for sure.

According to psychologist Sonja Lyubomirsky, doing just five small acts of kindness a week can boost our moods, particularly if we do a variety of them all in one day. Doing acts of kindness stimulates us immediately, but the effects also last over time.

There are further benefits of being kind. Helping others increases energy, self-esteem, and a sense of mastery over life, according to a study at Cornell University. That's because when we're helpful, we become more aware of our strengths and talents, and this helps us feel good about ourselves. Kindness begets kindness, and people pass it on.

> Regularly helping others on a close personal basis . . . resembles the experiences brought on through relaxation-type exercises, with their important stress reduction and health benefits. I can "prescribe" volunteering to patients as a way to control stress.
>
> —Herbert Benson, MD

It strengthens our immune system and boosts our health. Antibodies in the nose and mouth that fight off viruses are increased, according to researchers at Harvard. Students were asked to watch a video of Mother Teresa nurturing the needy in Calcutta, India. Even the most cynical undergraduates, who'd dismissed the nun's charitable work, showed an increase in immune function. Their white blood cells known as T cells, which are related to immunity and linked to longer life expectancy, were up. Amazing. By just watching someone show kindness, our immune system becomes activated.

Kind acts can also help with the experience of pain. Allan Luks, author of *The Healing Power of Doing Good*, studied the effects of kindness on three thousand individuals and called this phenomenon the "helper's high." The side effects of kindness include:

- Reduced feelings of depression

- Less hostility and isolation

- Increased optimism

Our neighbor was too old to pick up her morning newspaper from the front lawn, so as I rode my bike past to school I stopped and did it for her. Now, every day I make a point of helping her in some way, and it makes me feel better about myself.

—Jeremy, age 10

■ Greater joyfulness

■ More resilience

Kindness doesn't have to take any time or money, nor does it always require much effort. It can be as simple as opening a door for someone with a smile. Remember: the smile you give is the one you get back.

MINDFUL
KINDNESS
PRACTICE

THE KINDNESS GAME
Make up a new game with your children called the Kindness Game. It goes like this: Say that from now on you are each going to do at least three acts of kindness per day. Talk to them about what these might be. For instance, helping a friend at school, cheering someone up who's having a bad day, offering to help with the chores, or telling someone he or she did a good job.

RANDOM ACTS OF KINDNESS
At mealtimes, in the car, during bath time, or as you're putting your children to bed, share with each other what kind acts you

did. How did being kind make them feel? Which acts made them feel the best? Ask them if they'd like to carry on doing kind things and, if so, what would they do?

THE PAPER CHAIN OF KINDNESS

If you have time, make a paper chain of kindness by getting different-colored paper and cutting it into one-inch-wide strips. Have your children write down their kind acts on the colored paper. Loop the strips together and see how long the paper chain grows. Hang it somewhere prominent and encourage everyone to look at it and feel proud of what they have achieved.

Reflections

As I was driving up to my house in Los Angeles one day, an elderly woman stood in the middle of the road waving her hands wildly at me to flag me down. I pulled over and asked how I could help. In a clear state of panic she told me, "My maid is in labor and I can't drive and I haven't been able to reach her family." I opened the back door of my car and said, "Let's go!" Out waddled the heavily pregnant woman. On her hip was a little boy about fifteen months old. I put the two of them into my car and raced to the hospital emergency room. As we rushed in, her water broke. She was placed on a gurney, and I was left holding the baby. As she moaned, I sat next to her filling out the paperwork, but I didn't even know her name. With the help of the nurses we filled everything in before they wheeled her into the delivery room. Having no idea how long the labor might take, I kissed her and told her not to worry, that I'd take her son back to my home. I left my phone number and address and asked the nurses to give it to the woman's husband when he arrived. I drove home carefully with the baby balanced between my legs. Oh dear, no car seat. I brought him into the house where my children were playing and sat him in Wyatt's playpen. For the next few hours we ate and played and danced and had the best time. At around ten o'clock that night, I began to feel a tinge of panic as it crossed my mind that maybe, just maybe, we'd acquired a new family member. Kurt gave me that raised-eyebrow look! Then the doorbell rang. It was them! I took the baby, and Kurt and the kids followed as we went outside to meet a truck filled to the brim with joyful relatives and the new daddy. The baby clung to me and cried, reluctant to leave. We all had a good laugh, and then his father took him gently. *"Gracias!"* was shouted happily as they set off to go. The father leaned out of the truck with a grin and shouted, "My wife had a boy! She says thank you so much."

We watched as the truck accelerated down the street, feeling pretty darn happy knowing that what we'd done was a good deed.

HELPING OTHERS EVERY DAY

Helping others makes us feel so good. Whenever we are kind to others, we are also being kind to ourselves. Expressions of kindness have extraordinary benefits. In fact, we become more compassionate even to ourselves. We forgive ourselves for our own flaws and remind ourselves of the natural goodness in our hearts.

We are as nourished by our actions as the recipients of our kindness are.

Accepting that we have the capacity to be kind allows us to go out into the world as adults with a sense of optimism and value. Learning to appreciate ourselves in this way builds confidence.

Having compassion for ourselves is an important trait for our development. We say to friends and family, "Don't be so hard on yourself," but how often do we apply that to ourselves? We need to forgive ourselves and not be so self-critical, and when we perfect that skill, we will end up being less critical of others. Researchers say that kindness is related to many other positive attributes, including:

> *Doing good makes you feel good.... This health improvement is a real and reliable phenomenon and works to improve physical and psychological health as well as enhancing feelings of spiritual well-being. . . . It is the process of helping, without regard to its outcome, that is the healing factor.*
> —Allan Luks

- Developing wisdom

- Activating personal initiative

- Stimulating curiosity

- Encouraging exploration

- Deepening happiness

- Engendering optimism

Just think: so many benefits from a few simple acts of kindness.

17

Living a More Mindful Life

*Training is seen as important for strength, for physical
agility, for athletic ability, for musical ability—for everything
except emotions . . . but these are skills too, and are trainable
like any others.*

—Richard Davidson, PhD

I don't believe there is such a thing as a perfect parent. I know
that I'm still on my own journey of development and growth as a
human being, even though my children are now adults. All we
can hope is that our children experience more positive than negative effects from our parenting and become the healthy pilots
of their own lives. They will pass the legacy of our parenting to
their children and thus the ripple effect of positive growth
and transformation continues.

I hope that this book will help in ways that you never suspected and widen your perspective by opening some windows in
your mind. It is a sea chart with which to pilot your own voyage
to being your best self in order to be the best parent. There's a lot
of information to take in, and you may find it helpful to go over

some of it again, rereading chapters and reminding yourself of those practices that most help you and your children.

I hope that you will, at least, be able to find *ten mindful minutes every day* to harness some of the tips you have learned along the way. To set aside *five minutes twice a day* will help reduce your stress, renew your mind for clearer thinking, and create greater focus and connectivity with your children. It will be the time-out you need. Then you can help your children by discussing everything from breathing to relaxing the brain to gratitude and empathy.

Reflect for a moment on all that you have learned and experienced. Perhaps you've felt calmer in moments when your fear or anger was triggered. Maybe you've noticed that your children can actually sit still for a few minutes longer at a time and focus, or that they are sleeping better. Did you all feel happier as a result of thinking more optimistically or practicing gratitude? Do you enjoy mealtimes more?

Hang in there. Sometimes we slip up. Wrestling with ourselves, so to speak, is much harder sometimes than almost any task. Be patient with yourself. Two steps forward and one step back—this is the pattern of growth. Some practices may not have the effect you had hoped for. This is okay. Try something else. This isn't one size fits all; it is just a road map for you to follow.

YOUR TOOLBOX

Think of everything you have learned as tools in your own personal toolbox that you can use whenever you need them. The best way to keep any tool rust-free is to use it often.

Mindful Breathing

Continue to do mindful breathing on your own every day. Try to be consistent with your practice. Five minutes twice a day is ideal. Think of it like preparing an energy drink. Practice shorter periods of mindful breathing with your children. Of all the practices in this book, this is the core one, the "secret sauce" I mentioned earlier. Not only is it a wonderful stress reliever, but you'll be building greater control of the prefrontal cortex, strengthening impulse control, and increasing the ability to focus. Just before bed is a great time to practice, when your children are jacked up and need to calm down, but pick your moment—morning, noon, or night. Whatever works for you. P.S. You'll be amazed at the conversations that follow once their minds are freed.

■ Remind your children whenever they have a test or just before a game to breathe mindfully for a minute or so to create the calm focus that will increase their performance.

■ If for some reason you find it difficult to find that quiet corner for yourself, worry not. I have created quiet spaces in my car, on a plane, in a train, even waiting in line. Remember, mindfulness and mindful breathing go with you wherever you go.

Mindful Sensing

■ During meals, everybody slow down and mindfully taste your food. Keep it light and fun. Talk about different flavors with your children and encourage them to savor every mouthful. This is just an exercise to do for a few minutes at a time. People tend to go back to their old ways and that's fine, but every now and again you can bring them back to the practice to give them a barometer of what to do. Use that time to talk about what foods are good for us and what foods aren't.

■ Whenever your child is distracted and not paying attention to you, encourage him or her to use mindful listening. Sit quietly together and breathe. Keep the emphasis on bringing stillness to the mind. If your children are running around, arguing, or fighting, put on calming music to help change the mood. Classical music such as Mozart can create a more peaceful atmosphere. Try to have it playing around the house, especially at busy or fraught times, to keep everyone calm.

■ If your children are rushing through homework, encourage them to use their mindful breathing and mindful seeing. It is the perfect combination for focus. First the breathing calms them down, and then they can really look at each question and think before they answer. Remind them what is going on in their brains and how they need to get the Wise Old Owl to soothe the Guard Dog.

■ Use whatever opportunity you can to go on a nature walk or out into the backyard to look around with new focus. Play "I Spy" in the car.

■ When it's time for your children to brush their teeth at night, encourage them to do it with mindful awareness. Tell them to imagine every tooth getting cleaner and cleaner, whiter and whiter, with every brushstroke and how they are the caretaker of each little tooth.

Optimism

- Teach your children about the difference between the "jar half full" and the "jar half empty."

- Learn to take a positive perspective, no matter what the situation. This doesn't mean being a Pollyanna but being mindful that a positive approach to every encounter can be beneficial in all aspects of your life.

Happiness

- If your children are feeling sad, acknowledge them, listen to them; their sadness is as palpable as our own.

- Now change the tone. Ask them to tell you about the happiest day of their lives so far. Encourage them to really go into detail. Share the joy and memories with them and remind them to look at their Happy Wall or take out the family photo albums or their Happiness Box. Have fun remembering the happiness captured in the pictures or the good times each object represents. Sometimes that's all it takes to lift the mood.

- Whenever you feel like you're rushing through the day, take a few mindful breaths and pause just for a minute. Try to be in the present and see the beauty of that moment.

- Make sure you have *family time* without the distraction of devices like phones, computers, or televisions. Turn off the technology and connect with each other instead.

Gratitude

■ Take turns around the dinner table or in the car to say what you're thankful for. Make the experience fun and light.

■ When you tuck your children into bed, take the time to tell them one thing they did that day that was great.

■ Every now and again, write a list to remind yourself what you most love about your partner, as well as your children. Keep the list handy for those moments when they annoy or frustrate you, or when emotions are running high. It will put you in a more balanced state of mind and change your patterns of thinking. It will also stop negative feelings from escalating, which can be very damaging for everyone involved.

Anger

■ Help your children learn to recognize the signals when they begin to feel angry. Do they have a clenched jaw or a red face? Is their breathing shallow? Take a few deep breaths with them and remind them to relax because they won't make good decisions in this state of mind.

■ Make it a family rule, when *anyone* is having a meltdown, to play the Traffic Signal Game. Say "Red light," then stop, go to your quiet spot, and do some mindful breathing.

Sadness

- Encourage your children to talk about feelings. Let them know that it is all right to feel sad, and remind them that you feel sad sometimes, too.

- Help your children draw images or write about their sadness to help shift their perspective. The creative process of writing or drawing is very therapeutic in getting feelings out.

Fear

- It is good to discuss being fearful with your children. Just talking about what frightens them can help them move beyond it. Let them know that what they are feeling is entirely normal. Don't belittle or trivialize what they are feeling because it is still very real to them. Teach them how to rate it, on a scale of 1 to 10, and remind them that something that was a 10 a few months ago no longer scares them.

- Have your children write down any worries they have, then put them in a box with a lid that closes. Tell them that those worries have now been put away.

- When talking about anything that is troubling them at bedtime, attune your breathing to theirs, then have them name their fears or worries and let them go on each out breath. Try to help them think calming, positive thoughts just before they go to sleep.

Empathy

▪ Continue to use daily events to help children put themselves in other people's shoes, such as during sibling arguments or fights with friends. Remind them of different perspectives in the books they're reading or stories in the news.

▪ Create a list of mindful family rules and put it somewhere where everyone can see it. For instance: Treat one another the way you'd want to be treated. Help when others need help. Use the Traffic Signal Game when angry or frustrated. Sit quietly whenever you need to practice mindful breathing.

Kindness

▪ Encourage a culture of random acts of kindness. Talk about it with your children and encourage them to come up with different ways to be kind.

▪ Every now and again, make a new paper chain of kindness or add to the one you already have.

▪ Expand your kindness practice as part of a family culture. Volunteer in a soup kitchen, collect used clothes or toys for the needy, or sponsor a child in a developing country. Decide together which things you're going to do as a family and why.

▪ Try to be mindfully aware every day of your lives. The more your children see that this is the path you have chosen, the more they will copy your practices and develop their own ways to cope with life's challenges and be empathetic, compassionate, and kind.

*   *   *

I can't think of a greater way to become better parents than to nurture ourselves and our ability to be mindful to gain greater insight and understanding as to who we are as people. That's the way we become mindful parents, loving parents, effective parents, and—yes—joyful parents. It's an exciting journey to meet ourselves and sit quietly—to hear our own heartbeat. It's really the first step to peace. If a peaceful child can create a peaceful world, then a peaceful parent can create a peaceful child.

My heart goes out to all of you who are trying to learn more about yourself in order to be the best parent to your children. I've always believed that we and our children grow together. So open your hearts and minds to your personal discovery of who you are, what you want for your family, and how you can wholesomely achieve it.

As Jon Kabat-Zinn says, "Parenting is like a relay race in which you run alongside your child for the first eighteen years." At this point in their lives, you are still running, breathlessly trying to keep pace with their progress and yet be on hand to catch them if they fall.

This book is just the beginning. Your mind will flower and grow if you research further and dig deeper. There are so many brilliant minds out in the world right now ready to share with you the wonderful ways of developing mindfulness as a way of life. I honor the people who have done so much groundbreaking work. I am humbled by their expertise. I urge you to immerse yourself in their findings and take pieces of their brilliance into your heart.

Always remember that our children will never love anything

or anyone the way they love you. It's a relationship that's very deep and truly personal. I hope that the course I have set you on as you have journeyed through these pages will help create the happiest, healthiest connection between you and your children. Eventually, you will watch them run ahead of you, the baton of your loving legacy held tightly in their hands.

GLOSSARY

adrenaline: a stress hormone and neurotransmitter

amygdala: an almond-shaped structure that acts like a Guard Dog in the brain

cortical brain: also known as the "new brain," where our most critical thinking occurs

cortisol: the primary stress hormone, linked to everything from cancer to heart disease

dopamine: a "feel-good" neurotransmitter that acts on the sympathetic nervous system

executive functions: thinking, planning, reasoning, problem solving, decision making, and impulse control—or most of what we think of as intelligence

fMRI scan: functional brain imaging to demonstrate the function and status of the brain

hippocampus: part of the limbic system that helps with memory and spatial navigation

limbic brain: also known as the emotional brain, a key area for emotions, long-term memory, and behavior

meditation: from the Latin meaning "to ponder," a form of holistic practice to cultivate and quiet the mind

metacognition: knowing about knowing; being able to analyze our actions and act accordingly

mindfulness: the practice of being mindful of one's awareness, feelings, and senses

mirror neurons: neurons that fire both when we act and when we observe

neurogenesis: the process by which new neurons are generated

neurons: specialized nerve cells in the brain that control storage and processing of information and are stimulated by electrical impulses and chemicals

neuroplasticity: the growth of new neural connections

neurotransmitters: brain chemicals that transmit information from nerves to cells via gaps or junctions known as synapses

positive psychology: a branch of psychology that focuses on enhancing strengths, the practice of gratitude and kindness, and the positive aspects of our state of mind

prefrontal cortex (PFC): the Wise Old Owl at the front of the brain, where our higher or critical thinking occurs

pruning: the process by which the brain prunes old neural connections it isn't using anymore

reptilian brain: the oldest part of our brain, also known as the "Stone Age brain"; manages our automatic responses, such as eating and breathing

resonance: the way in which we give our full focused attention to attune to somebody's feelings so that they feel safe, understood, and connected

right and left hemisphere: the two halves of the cerebral brain, linked by the corpus callosum

social and emotional learning: how we cope day to day with thoughts, feelings, emotions, and our connections to others

secure attachment: the crucial emotional connection between children and adults that allows children to feel safe

synapse: the junction or gap between a neuron and a brain cell, crossed by neurotransmitters and electrical signals

REFERENCES

*Reading is equivalent to thinking with someone
else's head instead of with one's own.*

—Arthur Schopenhauer

Albers, Susan. *Eat, Drink, and Be Mindful.* New Harbinger, 2003.

Amen, Daniel G. *Making a Good Brain Great.* Random House, 2005.

Baraz, James, and Shoshana Alexander. *Awakening Joy.* Bantam Dell, 2010.

Bays, Jan Chozen. *Mindful Eating.* Shambhala, 2009.

Begley, Sharon. *Train Your Mind, Change Your Brain.* Ballantine Books, 2007.

Benard, Bonnie. *Resiliency: What We Have Learned.* WestEd, 2004.

Benson, Herbert. *The Relaxation Response.* Avon Books, 2000.

Boniwell, Ilona. *Positive Psychology in a Nutshell.* PWBC, 2008.

Brooks, Robert, and Sam Goldstein. *The Power of Resilience.* McGraw Hill, 2004.

___. *Raising Resilient Children.* McGraw Hill, 2001.

Carr, Nicholas. *The Shallows.* Atlantic, 2010.

Csikszentmihalyi, Mihaly. *Flow.* Harper and Row, 1990.

The Dalai Lama and Paul Ekman. *Emotional Awareness.* Henry Holt, 2008.

Davidson, Richard J., ed. *Anxiety, Depression, and Emotion.* Oxford University Press, 2000.

Dyregrov, Atle. *Grief in Children.* Jessica Kingsley, 2008.

Ekman, Paul, and Richard J. Davidson, eds. *The Nature of Emotion.* Oxford University Press, 1995.

Elias, Maurice J., Steven E. Tobias, and Brian S. Friedlander. *Emotionally Intelligent Parenting.* Three Rivers Press, 1999.

Emmons, Robert A. *Thanks!* Houghton Mifflin, 2007.

Emmons, Robert A., and Michael E. McCullough, eds. *The Psychology of Gratitude.* Oxford University Press, 2004.

Fredrickson, Barbara L. *Positivity.* Crown, 2009.

Gallwey, W. Timothy. *The Inner Game of Work.* Random House, 2001.

Gazzaniga, Michael S., ed. *The Cognitive Neurosciences,* 4th Edition. MIT Press, 2009.

Goleman, Daniel, narr., *Destructive Emotions.* Bantam Books, 2003.

___. *Emotional Intelligence.* Bantam Books, 1995.

Gottman, John. *Raising an Emotionally Intelligent Child.* Prentice Hall and IBD, 1998.

Gottman, John, and Nan Silver. *The Seven Principles for Making Marriage Work.* Crown, 1999.

Greenland, Susan Kaiser. *The Mindful Child.* Free Press, 2010.

Hart, Leslie A. *Human Brain and Human Learning.* Longman, 1983.

Healy, Jane M. *Endangered Minds.* Simon and Schuster, 1999.

___. *Your Child's Growing Mind.* Broadway Books, 2004.

Kabat-Zinn, Jon. *Coming to Our Senses.* Hyperion, 2005.

Kabat-Zinn, Myla, and Jon Kabat-Zinn. *Everyday Blessings.* Hyperion, 1997.

Kagan, Jerome, and Nancy Snidman. *The Long Shadow of Temperament.* Belknap Press, 2004.

Kehoe, John. *The Practice of Happiness,* Zoetec Books, 2001.

Lantieri, Linda. *Building Emotional Intelligence.* Sounds True, 2008.

Levine, Madeleine. *The Price of Privilege.* Harper, 2008.

Levy, Aharon, Ettie Grauer, David Ben-Nathan, and E. Ronald de Kloet, eds. *New Frontiers in Stress Research.* Harwood Academic Publishers (The Netherlands), 1998.

Louv, Richard. *Last Child in the Woods.* Atlantic Books, 2010.

Luks, Allan. *The Healing Power of Doing Good.* iUniverse.com, 2001.

Lyubomirsky, Sonja. *The How of Happiness.* Sphere, 2007.

Mayes, Linda C., and Donald J. Cohen. *The Yale Child Study Center Guide to Understanding Your Child.* Little, Brown, 2002.

Peterson, Christopher. *A Primer in Positive Psychology.* Oxford University Press, 2006.

Pinker, Steven. *How the Mind Works.* W. W. Norton, 1999.

Prochnik, George. *In Pursuit of Silence.* Doubleday, 2010.

Reivich, Karen, and Andrew Shatté. *The Resilience Factor.* Broadway Books, 2002.

Reznick, Charlotte. *The Power of Your Child's Imagination.* Perigee Books, 2009.

Ryan, M. J. *The Happiness Makeover.* Broadway Books, 2005.

Salzberg, Sharon. *The Force of Kindness.* Sounds True, 2005.

Sapolsky, Robert M. *Why Zebras Don't Get Ulcers.* Henry Holt, 2004.

Seligman, Martin E. P. *Authentic Happiness.* Free Press, 2002.

___. *Learned Optimism.* Vintage, 2006.

___. *The Optimistic Child.* Mariner Books, 2007.

Siebert, Al. *The Resiliency Advantage.* Berrett-Koehler, 2005.

___. *The Survivor Personality.* Perigee Books, 2010.

Siegel, Daniel J. *The Developing Mind.* Guilford Press, 1999.

___. *The Mindful Brain.* W. W. Norton, 2007.

___. *Mindsight.* Bantam Books, 2010.

Siegel, Daniel J., and Mary Hartzell. *Parenting from the Inside Out.* Jeremy P. Tarcher, 2003.

Small, Gary, and Gigi Vorgan. *iBrain.* Collins, 2008.

The Subject Centre for Information and Computer Sciences, University of Ulster and Loughborough University, United Kingdom. www.ics.heacademy.ac.uk.

Ury, William. *Getting Past No.* Random House, 1992.

Vaughan, Susan C. *Half Empty, Half Full.* Harcourt, 2000.

Williams, Mark, John Teasdale, Zindel Segal, and Jon Kabat-Zinn. *The Mindful Way Through Depression.* Guilford Press, 2007.

Willis, Judy. *How Your Child Learns Best.* Sourcebooks, 2008.

Wilson, Timothy D. *Strangers to Ourselves.* Belknap Press, 2002.

Wolfe, Patricia. *Brain Matters.* Association for Supervision and Curriculum Development, 2001.

BIBLIOGRAPHY

Angier, Natalie. 2009. Brain is a co-conspirator in a vicious stress loop. *New York Times*, August 17.

Aziz-Zadeh, Lisa, Tong Sheng, and Anahita Gheytanchi. 2001. Common premotor regions for the perception and production of prosody and correlations with empathy and prosodic ability. *PLoS ONE* 5(1): e8759 DOI: 10.1371/journal.pone.0008759.

Boylan, J. Gabriel. Torch in the ear. Bookforum.com, April/May 2010, www.bookforum.com/inprint/017_01/5375.

Bradbury, T. N., and F. D. Fincham. 1990. Attributions in marriage: Review and critique. *Psychological Bulletin* 107: 3–33.

Brown, K. W., and J. D. Creswell. 2007. Mindfulness: Theoretical foundations and evidence for its salutary effects. *Psychological Inquiry* 18: 211–37.

Bryant, F., and J. Veroff. 2006. *Savoring: A new model of positive experience*. Englewood Cliffs, NJ: Lawrence Erlbaum Associates.

Bushman, Brad, and C. A. Anderson. 2009. Comfortably numb: Desensitizing effects of violent media on helping others. *Psychological Science* 21(3): 273–77.

Davachi, L., J. P. Mitchell, and A. D. Wagner. 2003. Multiple learning mechanisms: Distinct medial temporal processes build item and source memories. *Proceedings of the National Academy of Sciences* 100(4): 2157–62.

Diamond, Adele. 2008. Neuroscience and education: Direct relevance of recent scientific discoveries to educational practice. Public address, "The Impact of Neuroscience on Society," Collège de France, Paris.

Eriksson, Peter S., et al. 1998. Neurogenesis in the adult human hippocampus. *Nature Medicine* 4: 1313–17.

Fanselow, M. S., and R. Ponnusamy. 2008. The use of conditioning tasks to model fear and anxiety. In *Handbook of anxiety and fear*, ed. R. J. Blanchard, D. C. Blanchard, G. Griebel, and D. Nutt, 29–48. The Netherlands: Elsevier Press.

Garrison Institute. 2005. *Contemplation and education: Current status of programs using contemplative techniques in K–12 educational settings: A mapping report.* www.garrisoninstitute.org/index.php?option=com_docman&task=doc_download&gid=56&Itemid=66.

Gould, Elizabeth, et al. 1997. Neurogenesis in the dentate gyrus of the adult tree shrew is regulated by psychosocial stress and NMDA receptor activation. *Journal of Neuroscience* 17: 2492–98.

Gourineni, Ramadevi, et al. 2009. Effects of meditation on sleep in individuals with chronic insomnia. Paper presented at "SLEEP 2009, the 23rd Annual Meeting of the Associated Professional Sleep Societies," Seattle, WA (Abstract ID: 0874).

Greeson, Jeffrey M. 2009. Mindfulness research update, 2008. *Complementary Health Practice Review* 14(1): 10–18.

Harrison, Y., and J. A. Horne. 2000. The impact of sleep loss on decision making: A review. *Journal of Experimental Psychology: Applied* 6: 236–49.

Henig, Robin Marantz. 2009. The anxious mind. *New York Times Magazine*, October 4, 2009.

Jacob, T. J. C., C. Fraser, L. Wang, W. E. Walker, and S. O'Connor. 2003. Psychophysical evaluation of responses to pleasant and malodor stimulation in human subjects: Adaptation, dose response and gender differences. *International Journal of Psychophysiology* 48: 67–80.

Jensen, B., and M. Harris. 2008. The learning environment and organisation of schools. *Education at a Glance, 2008*. Organisation for Economic Co-operation and Development (OECD), www.oecd.org/dataoecd/8/28/41271863.pdf.

Jensen, Eric. 1996. *Brain-compatible learning.* International Alliance for Learning, vol. 3, no. 2.

Jha, Amishi P., Elizabeth A. Stanley, and Michael J. Baime. 2010. What does mindfulness training strengthen? Working memory capacity as a functional marker of training success. In *Assessing mindfulness and acceptance processes in clients: Illuminating the theory and practice of change,* ed. Ruth A. Baer. Oakland, CA: New Harbinger Press.

Joëls, M., and T. Z. Baram. 2009. The neuro-symphony of stress. *Nature Reviews Neuroscience* 10: 459–66.

Kempermann, Gerd, and Fred H. Gage. 1999. New nerve cells for the adult human brain. *Scientific American* 280: 48–53.

Kliff, Sarah. 2007. This is your brain on optimism. *Newsweek* Web Exclusive, October 24, 2007.

Langer, E. J., and J. Rodin. 1976. The effects of choice and enhanced personal responsibility for the aged: A field experiment in an institutional setting. *Journal of Personality and Social Psychology* 134: 191–98.

Lutz, Antoine, Lawrence L. Greischar, Nancy B. Rawlings, Matthieu Ricard, and Richard J. Davidson. 2004. Long-term meditators self-induce high-amplitude gamma synchrony during mental practice. *Proceedings of the National Academy of Sciences* 101(46): 16369–73.

Maclin, Amy. 2010. Your hormones and weight loss: How to find balance. Wholeliving.com. www.wholeliving.com/article/balanced-weight-loss.

Mayer, J. D., P. Salovey, and D. R. Caruso. 2004. Emotional intelligence: Theory, findings, and implications. *Psychological Inquiry* 15: 197–215.

Neff, K. D., S. S. Rude, and K. L. Kirkpatrick. 2007. An examination of self-compassion in relation to positive psychological functioning and personality traits. *Journal of Research in Personality* 41: 908–16.

Neville, Helen J., and Daphne Bavelier. 2000. Specificity and plasticity in neurocognitive development in humans. In *The cognitive neurosciences,* ed. M. S. Gazzaniga, 83–99. Cambridge, MA: MIT Press.

Optimism and your health, *Harvard Men's Health Watch,* May 2008.

Saczynski, J. S., et al. 2010. Depressive symptoms and risk of dementia. *Neurology* 75(1): 35–41.

Shapiro, Shauna, Gina Beigel, Kirk Warren Brown, and Christine M. Schubert.

2009. Mindfulness-based stress reduction for the treatment of adolescent psychiatric outpatients: A randomized clinical trial. *Journal of Consulting and Clinical Psychology* 77(5): 855–66.

Sharot, T., T. Shiner, A. C. Brown, J. Fan, and R. J. Dolan. 2009. Dopamine enhances expectation of pleasure in humans. *Current Biology* 24(19): 2077–80.

Shriver, Timothy P., and Roger P. Weissberg. 2005. No emotion left behind. *New York Times*, August 16, 2005.

Strayer, David L., and William A. Johnston. 2001. Driven to distraction: Dual-task studies of simulated driving and conversing on a cellular telephone. *Psychological Science* 12 (November).

Suttie, Jill. 2007. Mindful kids, peaceful schools. *Greater Good* (summer 2007): 28–31.

University of California, Irvine. 2008. Short-term stress can affect learning and memory. *Science Daily* (March 13). www.sciencedaily.com/releases/2008/03/080311182434.htm.

Wallis, Claudia. 2005. The new science of happiness. *Time*, January 17, 2005.

Weissberg, R. P., and K. Kumpfer, eds. 2003. Prevention that works for children and youth. *American Psychologist* 58: 425–32.

Willander, Johan, and Maria Larsson. 2007. Olfaction and emotion: The case of autobiographical memory. *Memory & Cognition* 35(7): 1659–63.

Williams, J. M. G. 2008. Mindfulness, depression and modes of mind. *Cognitive Therapy and Research* 32: 721–33.

Willis, Judy. 2007. Neuroscience of joyful education. ASCD: Educational Leadership Online, vol. 64. www.ascd.org/publications/educational-leadership/summer07/vol64/num09/The-Neuroscience-of-Joyful-Education.aspx.

Wilmes, Barbara, Lauren Harrington, Patti Kohler-Evans, and David Sumpter. 2008. Coming to our senses: Incorporating brain research findings into classroom instruction. *Education* 128(4): 659–66.

ACKNOWLEDGMENTS

There are so many people to thank not only for helping me with my book but also for inspiring me to take the initiative to travel down this exciting new path. A special thanks to the parents who led me to writing this book and to the children who are a constant wellspring of potential, igniting my enthusiasm for helping our children thrive.

To the many skilled educators, psychologists, research scientists, mindfulness practitioners, and neuroscientists whose work has so inspired me and taught me so much, my sincere thanks.

But the following deserve special mention for their patience, generosity of spirit, and compassion. So to Daniel Siegel, Kim Schonert-Reichl, Amishi Jha, Jon Kabat-Zinn, Susan Kaiser Greenland, Daniel Goleman, Janice Parry, Jen Erickson, Marc Meyer, and all those at Scholastic: I thank you from the bottom of my heart.

Thanks also to Alan Nevins, my patient and dedicated agent; John Duff, my publisher who believed in and supported this book; and Wendy Holden, whose words string together like precious pearls.

INDEX

Page numbers in *italic* indicate illustrations.

ABOUT THE AUTHOR

Goldie Hawn is the founder of the Hawn Foundation as well as an international children's advocate and enthusiastic campaigner for the mindful celebration of life. An Academy Award–winning actress, producer, and director, she is also a mother and grandmother. Her bestselling autobiography, *A Lotus Grows in the Mud*, was published in 2005.

Wendy Holden is an author of more than twenty-five books, including a novel. A former newspaper journalist and foreign correspondent, she cowrote Goldie Hawn's autobiography and specializes in writing books about remarkable women.

ABOUT THE HAWN FOUNDATION
AND MINDUP

The Hawn Foundation seeks to help transform children's lives by providing them with opportunities to acquire vital social and emotional skills to improve academic performance, enhance the quality of their lives, and help others in their community. We support research studies conducted by university-associated social scientists and neuroscientists and develop evidence-based educational programs for children, such as MindUP, using cutting-edge scientific research on the brain and social and emotional learning. The Hawn Foundation is committed to helping children lead confident, happy, and successful lives. We also assist educators in creating supportive learning and social environments that effectively address children's mental and physical well-being while nurturing the growth of creative, reflective habits of mind.

MindUP promotes a kind of unwritten code for mindful conduct for children of all ages in and out of the classroom. The keystone of this ambitious educational initiative, it is an internationally successful, curriculum-friendly program that harnesses the latest developments in neuroscience, educational expertise, and parental common sense to create optimism, well-being, and emotional balance. By teaching children the function and beauty of their own brains, they are put in the driver's seat and given the emotional and cognitive tools to help them manage behavior, reduce stress, sharpen concentration, and increase empathy and, ultimately, joy.

www.thehawnfoundation.org/mindup